Comments on other *Amazing Stories* from readers & reviewers

"*Tightly written volumes filled with lots of wit and humour about famous and infamous Canadians.*"
Eric Shackleton, *The Globe and Mail*

"*The heightened sense of drama and intrigue, combined with a good dose of human interest is what sets* Amazing Stories *apart.*"
Pamela Klaffke, *Calgary Herald*

"*This is popular history as it should be... For this price, buy two and give one to a friend.*"
Terry Cook, a reader from Ottawa, on **Rebel Women**

"*Glasner creates the moment of the explosion itself in graphic detail...she builds detail upon gruesome detail to create a convincingly authentic picture.*"
Peggy McKinnon, *The Sunday Herald*, on **The Halifax Explosion**

"*It was wonderful...I found I could not put it down. I was sorry when it was completed.*"
Dorothy F. from Manitoba on **Marie-Anne Lagimodière**

"*Stories are rich in description, and bristle with a clever, stylish realness.*"
Mark Weber, *Central Alberta Advisor*, on **Ghost Town Stories II**

"*A compelling read. Bertin...has selected only the most intriguing tales, which she narrates with a wealth of detail.*"
Joyce Glasner, *New Brunswick Reader*, on **Strange Events**

"*The resulting book is one readers will want to share with all the women in their lives.*"
Lynn Martel, *Rocky Mountain Outlook*, on **Women Explorers**

AMAZING STORIES

TORONTO MAPLE LEAFS

AMAZING STORIES

TORONTO MAPLE LEAFS

Stories of Canada's Legendary Team

HOCKEY

by Jim Barber

PUBLISHED BY ALTITUDE PUBLISHING CANADA LTD.
1500 Railway Avenue, Canmore, Alberta T1W 1P6
www.altitudepublishing.com
1-800-957-6888

Copyright 2004 © Jim Barber
All rights reserved
First published 2004

Extreme care has been taken to ensure that all information presented in this book is accurate and up to date. Neither the author nor the publisher can be held responsible for any errors.

Publisher	Stephen Hutchings
Associate Publisher	Kara Turner
Editor	Joan Dixon

We acknowledge the financial support of the Government of Canada through the Book Publishing Industry Development Program (BPIDP) for our publishing activities.

Altitude GreenTree Program
Altitude Publishing will plant twice as many trees as were used in the manufacturing of this product.

National Library of Canada Cataloguing in Publication Data

Barber, Jim (Jim Christopher Matthew)
Toronto Maple Leafs / Jim Barber.

(Amazing stories)
Includes bibliographical references.
ISBN 1-55153-788-5

1. Toronto Maple Leafs (Hockey team)--History.
I. Title. II. Series: Amazing stories (Canmore, Alta.)

GV848.T6B29 2004   796.962'64'09713541   C2004-903746-3

Amazing Stories® is a registered trademark of Altitude Publishing Canada Ltd.

Printed and bound in Canada by Friesens
2 4 6 8 9 7 5 3

To the former players, coaches, managers, and most importantly, to the fans of the Toronto Maple Leafs — past, present, and future. We hope you enjoy these amazing stories of one of Canada's most important institutions.

Contents

Prologue 11
Chapter 1 The Budding of the Leafs 13
Chapter 2 The First Golden Age: 1946-51 27
Chapter 3 The Centennial Leafs: 1967 39
Chapter 4 So Close and Yet So Far: 1970s 54
Chapter 5 The Ugly Years: 1980s 68
Chapter 6 The Dougie Era: 1990s 81
Chapter 7 The Battle of Ontario: 2000-4 96
Bibliography 110

Prologue

The game was already well in hand but Doug Gilmour was still on the hunt, looking to add an exclamation mark to his fine evening's work. As he crossed the centre line, close to the boards on his right, he shifted into another gear. Perhaps he was feeling tired, or invincible. Dipping towards the middle of the rink, he put his head down as he looked for the puck in front of him.

"Don't put your head down!" novice, atom, and peewee coaches have cried throughout the ages, in their efforts to drill the mistake out of their players. Gilmour probably wished his coaches' cries had resonated a few milliseconds before he hit the Kings' blueline. At that line, ready to meet him, was six feet, two inches, and 220 pounds of bone, gristle, and bad attitude named Marty McSorley.

BAM!

Because he was much taller, McSorley caught Gilmour's head with his elbow, sending both his helmet and senses reeling. Like a rag doll that had been tossed into the air, Gilmour's limp body spun through the air, landing roughly on the ice. A huge, loud gasp rose from the crowd. Toronto Maple Leafs fans and players watched aghast as their star lay motionless for what seemed like an eternity. It was long enough for

Toronto Maple Leafs

teammate Wendel Clark's warrior instincts to take hold. He rushed towards McSorley, who had remained standing nearby, as if admiring his handiwork. If the purpose of the hit on Gilmour was to demoralize the Maple Leafs, to take the wind out of their sails, it had backfired. Clark's piston-like hands landed with bloody authority on McSorley's face, blackening and bloodying one eye.

The legendary Maple Leafs would not be intimidated.

Chapter 1
The Budding of the Leafs

The puck travelled so fast that no one in the rink saw it go in. Cecil "Babe" Dye had just scored the most famous of his invisible goals. The darling of Toronto hockey fans, Babe Dye was one of the most gifted players in the whole four-year-old National Hockey League (NHL). Although he had been a prolific goal scorer in the league for two seasons, he solidified his status in this 1922 series as the first playoff hero of Toronto professional hockey.

He scored the famous goal to help his team, the Toronto St. Patrick's, successfully challenge the Vancouver Millionaires of the Pacific Hockey League (PCHL) for the Stanley Cup. The Toronto team had already eliminated their arch rivals — and two-time defending Cup champions — the Ottawa Senators,

Toronto Maple Leafs

in the NHL playoffs. (In those days, the Stanley Cup was contested between the champions of the NHL and the PCHL.)

At the face-off held at the Vancouver blueline, the Toronto centreman, Reg Noble, had won the draw. Like any good centre, he drew it back to his favourite trigger man, Dye, who flicked his wrists as no one else could.

Vancouver goalie Hugh Lehman had looked like a crouched statue as the puck blew past him. Where was the puck? Referees and players from both teams skated around, confused as to its whereabouts. Only fans in the stands behind Lehman knew what had happened and were cheering loudly. It took a few more seconds for the goal to register with everyone else in the noisy building.

Babe Dye, with a grin from ear to ear, had already glided back to centre ice, where he took his position to await the dropping of the puck by the referee. "Finally, goalie Lehman and the officials spotted the puck in the twine in the Vancouver goal. They couldn't believe it had arrived there, almost unseen," recounted hockey historian Brian McFarlane.

With the goal, Dye's shooting prowess became even more legendary. His reputation was sealed in the 1922 Stanley Cup season, as an 18-year-old junior, when he scored 12 goals with his unique wrist shot — from his own side of the centre ice line. It was this potent and accurate shot that set Dye head and shoulders above the crowd and led to an NHL-record nine playoff goals in that Stanley Cup final series. While assists were not recorded as religiously as goals at that

The Budding of the Leafs

time, it was apparent that Dye wasn't much into passing anyway. The torque he generated clutching his solid hickory stick with his Popeye-like forearms was sufficient to propel the puck past any netminder. Dye credited his mother, of all people, with helping him develop this weapon.

Shortly after his birth in May 1898, Cecil Dye's father had died, leaving mother Essie to raise the youngster alone. Essie Dye decided that although her son was small of stature, he would be big in athletic accomplishments. Considered to be a pretty good athlete in her own right, she understood how it took practice and discipline to become proficient at any skill. Making sure Cecil completed his skating and shooting drills on the outdoor ice rink that she built for him, she did as much to help Babe as Walter did for Wayne Gretzky during his formative hockey years. When asked about his amazing ability to score goals from long distances, Dye apparently laughed out loud and said, "Aw, my mom could have scored those goals standing back on our goal line. And she can throw a baseball harder than I can."

Standing only five feet, eight inches tall, and rarely tipping the scales at more than 150 pounds, Dye may have been slight, but he was the typical all-round athlete in the days when top athletes in one sport could also excel at a number of others. (Lionel Conacher, Canada's premier athlete of the first half century, had been a hockey, football, lacrosse, and track star.) A native of Hamilton, the multi-talented Dye played football up the road as a halfback for the Toronto

Toronto Maple Leafs

Cecil "Babe" Dye

Argonauts. He was also scouted by the legendary manager of the Philadelphia Athletics, Connie Mack, who offered the quite amazing sum of $25,000 for Dye to play baseball. But becoming a major league baseball player would have meant giving up his dreams of playing major league hockey. To Dye, the ice proved more alluring than the ivy-covered walls of Wrigley or Ebbett's Fields. This was certainly good news for

The Budding of the Leafs

the St. Patrick's hockey club, as Dye became one of the cornerstones of the team's future success.

Dye wasn't a one-man show. For the first couple of years with the club, he was on a line with another future Hall-of-Famer, Reg Noble. Noble averaged nearly 20 goals per season through most of his time with the Toronto team. Even though he was a forward in Toronto, Noble was known as a versatile, tough-as-nails player. His skating ability distinguished him from Dye — Noble was able to get up and down the length of the rink fast enough to catch onrushing attackers. He was also quite a good stickhandler and, as his excellent record indicated, not a bad shot in his own right. His skating ability and defensive presence made him a natural for the blueline. The transition was fairly seamless as Noble became one of the league's most effective and feared defenders after he was traded to the Montreal Maroons, where he won his third Stanley Cup. Howie Morenz commented in the early 1930s, "There was no one tougher [to get the puck around] than Reg Noble."

But before Noble or Dye or any of the other early superstars who won the Stanley Cup with Toronto in 1922 were out of grammar school, professional hockey in North America had become increasingly sophisticated. The National Hockey Association (NHA), the predecessor of the current NHL, began play in 1910 after a wild first decade of major league hockey exploded with leagues, franchises, and outrageous players' salaries. Mining magnates and millionaire playboys had built Stanley Cup-contending teams in such remote locales as Pembroke, Haileybury, and Cobalt. When the owners and league managers returned to their senses, somewhat chastened and a lot poorer, they decided to form one big, solid professional league — the NHA. The Ottawa Senators and teams from Montreal and Quebec joined with two Toronto teams. One of them, dubbed the Blueshirts, quickly became the stronger of the two Toronto organizations, both on and off the ice.

The mercurial and principled owner of the Blueshirts, Eddie Livingstone, was a sports impresario who was concerned more about his team, the integrity of the game of hockey, and its fans than making a profit. Not nearly as wealthy as his counterparts in Montreal, Ottawa, and Quebec City, Livingstone had to rely on good scouting ability, solid management skills, and a lot of moxie to build his club. In 1914, he brought Toronto its first Stanley Cup.

Before the 1916-1917 campaign was halfway over, however, Livingstone found himself on the outside of the NHA league looking in. During the First World War, a team created from enlisted professionals had been part of the NHA. It was based in Toronto, like the Blueshirts. But when shipped overseas after only a handful of games, it left the Blueshirts as the only team in the league from Toronto.

Livingstone was always considered a rogue element, and the other NHA owners had been looking to get rid of him for a few years. Claiming it was too difficult to adjust the

The Budding of the Leafs

schedule and not economically feasible to travel to Toronto to play only one team, the NHA suspended the Blueshirts team from the league for the season. Its players were dispersed throughout the remaining teams with the understanding that the team would be welcomed back into the league for the 1917-1918 season. But by that time, the NHA was left with only one team, the Blueshirts.

The other governors of the NHA had decided to create a new league — the National Hockey League. Livingstone's team had been playing in the Arena Gardens, the largest rink in town and the only one with artificial ice. The owners of the arena were from Montreal. In the new Montreal-based NHL, the Toronto franchise was awarded to the Arena Gardens' owners. These owners had no intention of renting the ice to Livingstone and his league of one. The NHA was forced to fold. Livingstone, tragically, was never to return to big-league hockey. He was a seemingly good hockey man but was out-maneuvered in a game he couldn't win.

The players on Livingstone's Blueshirts roster were then rented to the Arena Gardens group and competed successfully in the first NHL season with no official name. They were known first as the Torontos and later dubbed the Arenas. The first year was tumultuous for the new league, and the regular season ended with only three active teams: Toronto, the Montreal Canadiens, and the Ottawa Senators — a three-way rivalry that would be re-ignited much later in the 1990s. The Arenas defeated Montreal, earning the city of Toronto its

Toronto Maple Leafs

first NHL championship. The team then went on to beat the Pacific Coast Hockey Association champions from Vancouver 3-2 in the best-of-five Stanley Cup championship series. Toronto now had its second Stanley Cup winner, in 1918.

After a couple of mediocre seasons, the team changed names, owners, and players to climb back atop the hockey world. In 1922, led by Babe Dye, the Toronto St. Patrick's team won the Stanley Cup title again. But the franchise began to flounder, spurring rumours of a sale and a move south of the border. Fortunately for Toronto, a feisty former military man entered the scene around the same time.

Constantine (Conn) Falkland Smythe had quite successfully managed junior, amateur, and university teams for years in Toronto. After also helping the fledgling New York Rangers assemble a formidable roster of talent for their inaugural campaign in the NHL, he was fired — ironically over Babe Dye. The owner wanted to acquire Dye as a drawing card for the Rangers. Smythe argued he was a selfish player whose skills were in decline. Smythe lost that battle — one of the few he lost in his career.

Conn Smythe decided then he needed a team of his own — he no longer wanted to be an employee controlled by a know-nothing owner. He planned to run all facets of his team on the fundamental tenets of sacrifice, teamwork, obedience, and effort that he honoured during his combat time in the First World War. The team that Conn Smythe set his sights on — the struggling St. Patrick's — was not exactly

The Budding of the Leafs

a winning proposition at the time. And the team already had an offer of approximately $200,000 from Philadelphia, ready to be signed. Showing a knack for negotiation that would stand him in good stead for much of the next three decades, Smythe convinced a number of Toronto businessmen to back his bid. He then convinced the St. Patrick's ownership group that it was their patriotic duty to sell the team to someone who would keep it in Toronto and make it the pride of the Dominion.

Smythe, an avid fan of horse racing, betting, and breeding, recognized when a filly such as the Toronto St. Patrick's had the potential to be in the winner's circle, both financially and on the score sheet. And he smelled both cash and glory when he looked at the possibilities of hockey in Toronto.

First, he decided the St. Patrick's was no longer a suitable name for the team he envisioned having broad national appeal. The Maple Leaf name came from Smythe's affinity for the logo on Canadian soldiers' uniforms during the war. He thought it would be a solid, patriotic name that would rouse the nationalistic fervour of fans from coast to coast. Hockey's popularity was growing beyond any one cultural or ethnic divide — and in his vision, it was ready to explode.

Smythe also felt that radio could be the medium to spread the excitement of hockey. He continued allowing a local radio station to broadcast the games, as it helped hockey attract a bigger following in the city. Much of this popularity was thanks to a squeaky-voiced radio announcer

Toronto Maple Leafs

who would invent hockey play-by-play.

Foster Hewitt had been a newspaper reporter in the sports department at the *Toronto Star* in 1923. One night in March, just as he was ready to head home from work, his boss asked him to go to the Mutual Street Arena to broadcast a hockey game over the newspaper's newly-acquired radio station, CFCA. Hewitt's nasal tone and excitable manner helped to bring the hockey games to life and inspired thousands of kids listening at home. Countless NHL players, broadcasters, and coaches credited their interest in hockey to Hewitt's radio broadcasts.

Smythe's vision of hockey's expanding popularity included the creation of a hockey palace — one whose size, grandeur, and architecture would rival that of great concert halls and opera houses. He saw the game as a form of theatre, a classy affair to which people would wear their Sunday best.

To fully realize his vision, Smythe needed a team that would be worthy of this proposed hockey palace. Gradually, he assembled the same sort of team as he had begun for the seemingly ungrateful Rangers. One of the holdovers from the St. Patrick's days was Clarence "Hap" Day, who would become as key to the success of the Maple Leafs as a coach and manager, as he was as a player. He was one of the best skating blueliners of his era and also one of the sneakiest. Foes would routinely claim he was holding their stick, but he was rarely caught.

The Budding of the Leafs

When Smythe took over the St. Patrick's team, Day continued as team captain even when its colours changed to blue and white, its name changed to the Maple Leafs, and its venue changed to the Maple Leaf Gardens. Day was Smythe's kind of player. A hard worker on the ice who led by example, he made a dynamic duo with King Clancy. The two of them struck fear into the hearts of defenders, not only for the way they controlled their own zone, but because Day could occasionally create havoc, via a nice pass or offensive rush, in the other team's end.

One of the other brilliant things Smythe did was to develop a feeder system by forging relationships with two local junior hockey programs. One was the St. Michael's Majors, based out of St. Michael's College, a private school in downtown Toronto run by the Basilian Fathers. The other was the Toronto Marlboros, also known as the Marlies. Catholic kids spotted by Smythe, or one of his ever-growing legion of bird-dogging scouts, would usually be assigned to St. Mike's. Protestant hopefuls would be put in the Marlie organization. The Marlies initially had the better program and graduated all three members of the famous Kid Line. Gentleman Joe Primeau came first, joining the Maple Leafs for the 1927-28 season. The following year, both Harvey "Busher" Jackson and Charlie Conacher, the younger brother of multi-sport star Lionel, joined Primeau.

This triumvirate of talent soon terrorized all opposition. Although unimposing in build, Primeau was a brilliant passer and skater who was able to make great plays at the most unlikely times. Conacher and Jackson would be called power forwards today. Both could skate and hit, both enjoyed the physical play, and both had hands that sent pucks past netminders with frightening regularity.

Other players came and went, but there were a few on whom Smythe counted to anchor his new team. Lorne Chabot, brought in from the New York Rangers, was ensconced in goal. He was guarded by a solid corps of defencemen including Hap Day and another Marlie, Reginald "Red" Horner, one of the toughest defencemen to ever play in the league. Before "Tiger" Williams, Wendel Clark, or Tie Domi, Horner was the Leafs' ultimate talented tough guy. What he lacked in speed he made up for with a pugnacious personality, a good first pass out of the zone, and a reputation as a fearsome body-checker and defender of his teammates.

One famous incident characterized Horner's impact on a game. On December 12, 1933, Boston Bruins defenceman Eddie Shore blasted Maple Leafs forward Ace Bailey with a devastating check. Critically injured, Bailey would never play hockey again. Horner immediately ensured Shore knew he had done a very bad thing — by cold-cocking him with one punch. Both Shore and Bailey were carted off the ice on stretchers.

The final piece of Smythe's championship team came in the form of an impish Irishman who would become a fixture around Maple Leaf Gardens well into the 1980s — Francis

The Budding of the Leafs

"King" Clancy. Smythe had to raid the rival Ottawa Senators for the player whom he called "one of the best defencemen in the league but also one of the most colourful." As the Senators' most marketable commodity, Clancy had been made available when the franchise ran into financial difficulties during the Great Depression. In exchange, the Senators wanted only a couple of decent players and a whole lot of cash. The team that had been one of the NHL's founding franchises, winning four Stanley Cups in the 1920s, would eventually bow out of the league for one season and then fold for what seemed for good. And that process began in earnest when the Senators let one of their best players go to Toronto.

Even though he was an Ottawa boy, Clancy wanted to play where he was needed. Smythe welcomed this plucky blueliner who would hit, shoot, score, and fight — the first three quite successfully. Clancy was known to tangle with anyone, even if they were bigger, stronger, or smarter. Although he lost most of his fights, he gained respect around the league for his showmanship, pluck, and heart. He was also a superstar in the league and would be a strong drawing card for the new hockey building that Smythe was planning for the corner of Church and Carlton Streets in Toronto. To help pay for Clancy, Smythe called on his horse and gambling instincts. He bought an untested horse called Rare Jewel for $250, then bet on it and won part of the $35,000 he needed to pay the Senators.

Smythe also gambled that he could build Maple Leaf

Toronto Maple Leafs

Gardens with limited funds, in the middle of the Depression, and in five months. He and his able assistant, Frank Selke, twisted the arms of bankers and businessmen. They also approached trade unions to accept a combination of cash and stock. Amazingly, the building was completed in time for the 1931-1932 NHL season.

On opening night, November 12, 1931, 13,233 fans jammed into Maple Leaf Gardens in time to hear the 48th Highlanders pipe the proceedings to order. Most of the fans looked as though they were dressed for a night at The Cotton Club, and not to see a bunch of sweaty small-town hockey players bash one another around the ice. While that year's team had some ups and downs, including the replacement of coach Art Duncan by Dick Irvin, the end of the season saw the new Maple Leaf Gardens christened the only way Smythe would have felt was satisfactory — with a Stanley Cup victory.

With the Kid Line pacing the attack and Clancy, Horner, and Day keeping the high-scoring Rangers stars at bay, the Maple Leafs won the 1932 Stanley Cup series in three straight games.

The team would make it to the finals a number of times in the 1930s, but it would take a decade — and a miracle — for the Toronto hockey faithful (now fully converted to the Maple Leaf forever) to cheer another Stanley Cup win.

Chapter 2
The First Golden Age: 1946-1951

One of the most dramatic episodes in the annals of hockey history took place during the 1941-42 NHL season. After the first three games of the Stanley Cup finals, the moribund Toronto Maple Leafs found themselves down three games to none. Coach Hap Day's charges were dispirited and seemed to lack the fire to come back against the underdog Detroit Red Wings.

Before the start of game four at Detroit's Olympia, the Leafs coach found a special motivational tool to bring into the dressing room. Player Bob Davidson recalled the legendary day: "Aside from some player changes, two things happened to get us in that winning mood ... First, Jack Adams, the Detroit manager, went on radio and said his team would wrap

Toronto Maple Leafs

it up in four games. He sounded pretty cocky and it made us mad. Then Hap Day, our coach, read us a letter from a little girl in Toronto, who said she'd be ashamed to go to school the next day if we lost four straight games in the finals."

Game four was a hard-fought 4-3 win for the Leafs while game five embarrassed the Red Wings 9-3. The sleeping giant had awakened. The team that had been favoured to win the series, and the Cup, was finally on a roll. Led by its captain, Syl Apps, and its goaltender, Walter "Turk" Broda, who earned a shutout in the series-tying game, the Leafs completed the miracle with a 3-1 triumph in game seven. After half a dozen tries to win another Cup since their inaugural season in the Gardens, the Leafs were finally back on top of the hockey world. It was an achievement fittingly completed in the "House that Smythe Built," before its largest crowd to date.

The remainder of the 1940s, besides being dominated by the mayhem of the Second World War, was also dominated by a Maple Leafs team that was always hoisting Lord Stanley's silver cup. The team that won an improbable Stanley Cup in 1942 with one of the greatest comebacks in sports history also managed to win the 1945 Cup with an inspired, but patchwork, roster.

After a very short rebuilding period, team management had hit upon a winning formula. Combine grizzled veteran talent, with all its experience and wisdom, with youthful vigour and often bone-crunching energy to create a cohesive unit. That was the successful mixture that brought Toronto

The First Golden Age: 1946-51

consecutive Stanley Cups in 1947, 1948, and 1949. Composed and conducted by the master impresario, team owner and manager Conn Smythe, the winning symphony of hockey talent included not just Apps and Broda from the 1942 Stanley Cup team, but famous stars Bashin' Bill Barilko and Theodore "Teeder" Kennedy.

Bill Barilko was slightly bigger than the average NHLer of his day at 5 feet, 11 inches, and 180 pounds. The scrappy youngster was born in Timmins, Ontario, in 1927 and had advanced from the mining leagues of Northeastern Ontario in the early 1940s to the glitz and glamour of Hollywood in the Pacific Coast Hockey League. His call to the big club came two-thirds of the way through the 1946-47 season.

Barilko made a name for himself as a punishing bodychecker who played the game with enthusiasm and, occasionally, reckless abandon — just the kind of player Conn Smythe wanted patrolling the blueline for his Maple Leafs. Along with the soon-to-be dubbed "Gold Dust Twins" (Gus Mortson and Jim Thomson), Barilko was part of the youngest blueline corps in the NHL. Mortson was one of his first admirers: he felt fortunate not to be on the receiving end of Barilko's hits. Instead, he watched his teammate's bodyslamming from the safety of the Maple Leafs bench. "I can still recall the biggest bodycheck I ever saw ... Bill Gadsby was playing for Chicago and he had the puck when he hit our blueline. But Barilko hit him just outside the line and they both went down. Barilko crawled on his hands and knees to

Toronto Maple Leafs

From left to right: Bill Ezinicki, Bill Barilko, and Ted Kennedy

get back to our bench. They had to get a stretcher, and carry [Gadsby] off ... there was no penalty, it was a good clean hit."

If not for a number of injuries to other players throughout the heart of the 1946-47 season, Barilko may never have made it from sunny California to two of Canadian hockey's most enduring institutions — the Toronto Maple Leafs and Maple Leaf Gardens. Mortson recalled, "We played about four

The First Golden Age: 1946-51

games and Bob Goldham, he got his arm broken. And then we had Garth Boesch, who played with him at that time, and he had a bad groin. And he kept pulling his groin all the time and so we played from about the first of November to almost the end of January with only three healthy defencemen," said Mortson. "They brought Barilko up from Hollywood. And he fit right in with what we had and what we needed."

Barilko's first NHL game came in early February of 1947, and his feistiness impressed teammate Howie Meeker to no end. "Holy jumpin' Jehosophat. The guy could hit and hit like a ton," he said. "Barilko gave us four mentally and physically tough defencemen whom you didn't want to go into the corner with. If you got any of them mad or came out of the corner with the puck, you were dead. Barilko was something else, a hard rock from the north."

There were, of course, other players on the ice making the Leafs successful. In the Maple Leafs goal stood the venerable and jocular Turk Broda. By the late 1940s, Broda was near the end of a long and illustrious playing career. One of the most popular Maple Leafs of his or any era, his infectious smile and fun-loving demeanour endeared him to reporters, fans, and teammates. He looked more like everyone's favourite uncle than a man who withstood barrages of rock-hard rubber on a nightly basis. Broda also appeared a lot thicker than his 5 feet, 9 inches, and 180 pounds. He had giant meat hooks for hands that looked as large as playing gloves. Although he was suspended by Smythe for a single game in

Toronto Maple Leafs

the 1949-50 season for being too chubby, he was really fit as a fiddle. How else would he have had a Hall of Fame career that featured a record of 302 wins, 62 shutouts, and a career goals-against average of 2.53? Broda also won five Stanley Cups and two Vezina Trophies.

Pressure never seemed to bother Broda. Like the best goaltenders of any era, the more important the game, the better he played. His happy-go-lucky façade hid a competitive fire that rages in the heart of any championship-calibre thoroughbred. Who knows what his career might have been had he not missed two complete seasons and most of a third — at his prime — answering his country's call of duty? Dozens of other NHL players, including Maple Leafs owner Conn Smythe and team captain Syl Apps, had enlisted in the Canadian Army during the Second World War.

A native of Paris, Ontario, Syl Apps was the captain of the Toronto Maple Leafs for much of the successful 1940s. He was not only idolized by hundreds of thousands of young hockey hopefuls for his grace and skill on the ice, he was admired by everyone who met him. Other Leafs captains like Doug Gilmour, Wendel Clark, and George Armstrong would also invoke feelings of respect and loyalty, but Apps' appearance in a room could create the buzz of a royal entrance. Because of his patrician bearing, he appeared taller than he was, yet his honest, self-effacing, and generous nature made him approachable. "He was as fine a man as has ever lived. There wasn't anybody cut from the same cloth as Syl Apps,"

The First Golden Age: 1946-51

his successor Teeder Kennedy has said. "Besides being a great player, he was as good a man as there was off the ice. He set a standard in a career that anyone would do well to follow." An all-around athlete, he finished sixth in the pole vault at the 1936 Olympic Games in Berlin. He was also a talented football and tennis player. Apps firmly believed in playing hard but clean. In the 1941-42 season, he played 38 games without any penalty minutes.

Because he was away at war, the captain Apps missed the 1945 playoffs. A rag-tag bunch of Maple Leafs upset Montreal and their famous Punch Line of Elmer Lach, Maurice "Rocket" Richard, and Toe Blake. Those three finished as the league's top three scorers as their team took first place — 28 points higher than Toronto. With guts, determination, and some luck, Toronto managed to shunt the Habs aside to face Detroit again in the finals.

After Toronto goalie Frank McCool, filling in during Broda's wartime absence, registered consecutive shutouts in the first three games in the series, it was now Toronto's turn to be the underdog. But, with memories of the famous 1942 comeback, the Red Wings started to fight. Although budding superstar Teeder Kennedy scored three times in the fourth game, the Leafs couldn't hold a 3-2 third period lead, eventually losing 5-3.

Detroit's goalie Harry Lumley took matters into his own gloves in the fifth game, shutting out Toronto 2-0 and then again 1-0 in the sixth contest. Panic threatened the Leafs

Toronto Maple Leafs

while the Detroit faithful rallied to avenge 1942. The seventh game was tense, as the teams traded goals heading into the third period. Babe Pratt was the hero of the day, scoring a few minutes after Detroit tied it at 1-1. He gave the Leafs a somewhat sheepish victory in the deciding game — and the Stanley Cup.

While Syl Apps was away serving in the war, the much younger Teeder Kennedy was just getting his feet wet in the professional game. He would become another of the greatest captains in the history of the team. Like his predecessor Syl Apps, Teeder Kennedy also inspired utter devotion from those playing alongside him, great respect from those playing against him, and incredible loyalty from Maple Leafs fans of all ages. He differed in his style of play and temperament from Apps, but that didn't seem to diminish the effectiveness of his game. "Teeder was more of a grinder. He wasn't an easy skater," said teammate, and later captain, Sid Smith. "I know that Teeder really looked up to Syl Apps and it just rubbed off on Teeder what Syl did and it just passed down and that's why they were both good captains."

Theodore Kennedy had been born in 1925 in the hard-working town of Port Colborne, where people seemed to have difficulty pronouncing his presidential-sounding name. It morphed from Teedore, to Teedor, ending up as Teeder. Conn Smythe appreciated people with hard-working pedigrees and called Kennedy the greatest Maple Leaf ever. Kennedy had to work for everything he got and would do

The First Golden Age: 1946-51

whatever was required of him to help his team win the game. Much like Darryl Sittler in the 1970s, he may not have been the most talented player on the Maple Leafs roster, but he certainly squeezed the most out of the talent he had. Howie Meeker said, "He was probably as great a competitor as has ever played the game and certainly ... the toughest competitor on our team. He had great hockey sense and great puck-handling and passing skills."

A focal point of the Leafs, Kennedy was also the focal point of the action — and the flashpoint of controversy — on a cold February evening in the opening round of the 1950 Stanley Cup finals. The Maple Leafs, the three-time defending champs, were winning the battle 5-0 in the Detroit Olympia against the Red Wings' Gordie Howe, "Terrible" Ted Lindsay, and Red Kelly.

Late in the contest, one of the greatest players of the game not only saw his career, but quite possibly his life, almost come to a premature end. As Gordie Howe tried to hit a surging Teeder Kennedy along the boards, he plunged head-first into the solid dasher at the top of the boards. Blood poured from his cracked skull.

Immediately, Detroit players assumed Kennedy was at fault. Team manager Jack Adams used the play as a rallying cry for his troops, who stormed back to tie the series. Detroit newspapers called for Kennedy's head, believing that Kennedy either tripped or butt-ended Howe deliberately. Toronto defended him: he was nothing more than an

Toronto Maple Leafs

innocent bystander. The incident remained a sore point with some of the Leafs players. Gus Mortson saw it from the ice, where he was about 10 feet behind Kennedy. "Howe had been coming across and was planning on hitting Kennedy from the side. He missed him and then hit the boards."

Howe had a deep cut over his eye, a broken nose and cheekbone, and a severe concussion — so severe that doctors had to operate for an hour and a half to relieve pressure on his brain. Kennedy took so much abuse in that game, and the rest of the series, that he became a shadow of his former self. Toronto had been expected to win the series fairly handily, but with their captain and inspirational leader battered, the team succumbed to the Wings in seven games. The winning goal came off a deflection — to the Leafs' great disappointment.

"We could have been the first team to win five [Stanley Cups] in a row." Mortson recalls. Then, in the sixth game, Mortson himself deflected a Wings shot into his own net, to lose the game. Unbelievably, in the final game, history repeated itself. "The puck hit Bill Barilko exactly where it hit me, and deflected into the net. So the one year, Barilko's the goat and the next year, he's the hero."

In the fifth and final game of the following year's Stanley Cup final series between the Toronto Maple Leafs and the Canadiens, it was indeed Barilko who played the hero in another famous Leafs moment. With his aw-shucks attitude and matinee-idol good looks, he sent the dressed

The First Golden Age: 1946-51

up crowd in Maple Leaf Gardens into a roaring state of near pandemonium. In the overtime period to end the tied game, Barilko and the rest of the Toronto defensive corps was told by head coach Joe Primeau not to get caught too deep in the Habs zone. He wanted them to avoid the possibility of a turnover that could lead to an odd-man rush going the other way. Mortson remembered Bill ignoring orders. "Bill, he must have gone in about 15 or 20 feet over the blueline. But he had this habit, when he started to make a rush for the puck like that, he would take two or three steps on his toes. And then he took a slap at the puck, and in this case, he sort of put himself in mid air," Mortson recalled. Sid Smith also remembered it clearly: "Bill just pinched in. That's something that was really a no-no in our day, for a defenceman to move in on the play like they do now." said Smith. "A defenceman in our day wasn't supposed to leave that point. And [Barilko] just took a gamble. If he didn't score, he would have got hell. But, anyway, it worked out good."

With the flying Bill Barilko the unlikely hero of the moment, the Toronto Maple Leafs had regained their position at the top — as the rightful possessors of the Stanley Cup. After the goal, an exuberant Barilko was swarmed by his teammates on the ice as flashbulbs lit the ice surface, capturing the important moment in sports history. No one knew at the time just how significant or poignant a photo it would make. Barilko wore one of the biggest grins ever seen in a post-game celebration — and for a hockey player, it was

Toronto Maple Leafs

an astonishingly complete, pearly-white grin. He held up a beverage to the news cameras as passing teammates tousled his hair.

A few months later, the boyish grin with its mischievous glint was missing somewhere in the dense scrub forests of Northern Ontario. "We really didn't think too seriously about it. We figured, 'well, they'll find him.'" said Mortson. "By training camp, they were still looking for him. They had half the navy and air force out looking for him." The wreckage of his plane was not found until 1962, 11 years later. For much of that time period, Barilko's team, the Toronto Maple Leafs, seemed to be lost in the wilderness as well.

Poor trades, bad luck, a sluggish farm system, and a vendetta against a burgeoning players' association consigned the Maple Leafs to also-rans for a good chunk of the 1950s. But while the Maple Leafs had been winning their impressive four Stanley Cups in five years, a number of younger players were patiently enduring their apprenticeships in the junior and minor pro ranks, preparing for prime time.

One of those youngsters was a strapping young strongman born in Cochrane, Ontario, not far from where Bill Barilko's remains were found. And, after playing four games with the Maple Leafs in 1951-52, this 22-year-old, rock-jawed blueliner named Tim Horton essentially took Barilko's spot on the Toronto Maple Leafs roster. He held on to it for 18 years, becoming a prime contributor to the team that would bring the memories of the glorious 1940s flooding back.

Chapter 3
The Centennial Leafs: 1967

The venerable old lady of Carlton Street, Maple Leaf Gardens, was awash in a sea of expectation. Since its construction in 1931, it had seen its share of powerful, memorable moments and held its share of championship glory. But there was something different about this evening of May 2, 1967.

The full house of 16,000 patrons must have known they were witnessing more than the climactic conclusion to another season of NHL hockey. It was more than a chance to wrap up another Stanley Cup championship: yes, there was a lot more to this than the sixth, and possibly clinching, game of the Stanley Cup finals between the Leafs and their long-time rivals, the Montreal Canadiens.

Whether they knew it or not, folks living in 1967 were

Toronto Maple Leafs

in the midst of major social and cultural change. Despite the fact that both Canada and the Maple Leafs team were getting older, Centennial Year was a time for youth and new ideas. Social and racial unrest were changing the way people thought and felt about their world — including the hockey world.

Sitting in the seats of a muggy Maple Leaf Gardens in their suits, hats, and eveningwear, fans were aware of the turmoil whirling around them. But they were happily distracted by what they had been witnessing on the ice. They didn't see hippies or sit-ins. They saw 40 clean shaven, short-haired hockey players, playing a game they'd played all their lives — a game that was as representative of Canada as the beaver. The average fan could identify more with these players than the social activists and draft-dodgers dominating the newspapers. The members of the Toronto Maple Leafs and Montreal Canadiens didn't earn much more money than the average person in the stands. These heroic figures, immortalized by Foster Hewitt on the radio and in weekend magazines across the nation, often had to take summer work to make ends meet.

In 1967, fans knew every player on every team. Of course, there were only six teams. Free agency was non-existent and rosters tended to change little from year to year. There was a certain level of comfort in the hearts and minds of hockey lovers knowing that Hull, Pilote, and Mikita would be playing for the Blackhawks; Howe, Delvecchio, and

The Centennial Leafs: 1967

Ullman for the Wings; Beliveau, Fergie, and the Pocket Rocket for the Habs.

But change and uncertainty was about to upset the comfort zone of the NHL fan. Before the next National Hockey League season began in six months, there would be unrest of a different sort. New teams would join the league. The landscape of the hockey world of the last quarter century would be inexorably altered. The league had plans to double its size, with the new teams located in such foreign locales as Oakland, Los Angeles, St. Louis, Philadelphia, Pittsburgh, and Minnesota.

These disturbing thoughts were put off for after the game and later in the off season. Back in a tense Maple Leaf Gardens, there were only 55 seconds remaining in regulation time. The Maple Leafs had a tenuous hold on their 2-1 lead. The Montreal Canadiens had been pressing for the equalizer for some time, and now the game was down to a critical face-off in the Maple Leafs zone. Favourites in this series, Montreal was supposed to bring the Stanley Cup back for display at Expo 67 — the World's Fair — already under way in Montreal.

There were now six skaters wearing the *bleu, blanc, et rouge* ready to pounce on the five Maple Leafs defenders plus the war-horse between the pipes, 38-year-old Terry Sawchuk. The Canadiens goalie, Lorne "Gump" Worsley, had been pulled for an extra attacker. Jean Beliveau, the classy captain of Montreal, was already waiting at the face-off dot to the left of Sawchuk.

The moment was the most vivid for stalwart 41-year-old Leafs blueliner Allan Stanley. "This is the last face-off of the sixth game. Punch [coach/manager Punch Imlach] is behind the bench, and he sends out Horton and [George] Armstrong, [Red] Kelly and [Bob] Pulford, and then he looked at me and said 'Stanley, you take the face-off.' So I gave him the double take, you know, I must have heard something wrong here. I looked at him again and he said, 'yeah, you take the face-off.'"

It wasn't that uncommon to see a defender take a face-off in a team's defensive zone at a critical juncture, but Stanley, by his own admission, had not taken such a draw in quite some time. "At one time, the defencemen always seemed to be bigger than the centreman," Stanley said. "And the play was, you made a pass at the puck and then ran the centreman out of there. I guess we did that so much they brought in a new rule that it was face-off interference."

Understandably nervous, Stanley slowly glided across the ice from the Maple Leafs bench, aware his teammates and opponents were watching closely from behind their respective bunkers, along with everyone in the building and millions at home. " I just took my time going out there. I thought, 'what the hell am I going to do out here,'" Stanley continued. "I was actually pretty good on face-offs. My anticipation was good, I knew when the referee was going to drop the puck. So I said, 'I'll have to do it the way I always do it.' So, I took one

The Centennial Leafs: 1967

pass at the puck and it happened to go back to Kelly on the edge of the circle. And then I took one stride and ran the stick between Beliveau's legs and ran him out of the play."

Technically, a penalty should have been called on Stanley, but Beliveau's protests went unheard, and the play was allowed to continue. "So the puck went back to Kelly, then went over to Pulford, he put it up to Armstrong who was going up the right wing at this time, and he skated in there and put the puck in the net. And while all of this was going on, Beliveau was chasing the referee, hollering 'face-off interference.'" But with 47 seconds left, the Leafs now led 3-1, and there was jubilation in the Gardens, in homes across Canada, and on the Maple Leafs bench.

And junior Leafs member Ron Ellis could finally breathe. He had been on the bench, nervously surveying the scene, when Stanley was ordered to take the draw. He knew that it would be a whole new game if Beliveau could win the draw and slide it back to one of his teammates who had a great shot on a probably-screened Sawchuk. For the 21-year-old Ellis, the 55 seconds equalled an eternity. "The overall feeling on the bench was that there was no problem at all," he said. "We had some confidence that the people on the ice, if we lost the draw, were certainly able to take care of the situation. But I know there was one guy who was pretty excited. His number was eight. That was me. For the majority of the team, this was potentially their fourth Stanley Cup in six years, so maybe they were not quite as excited."

Toronto Maple Leafs

Stanley, Kelly, Horton, Pulford, netminder Sawchuk, and team captain George Armstrong represented the old guard of a pretty old Toronto Maple Leafs team. By sending them out at this pivotal moment of the game, coach Imlach knew he was sending a quintet who wouldn't be unnerved by the gravity of the situation. They would make the right play, the smart play, no matter who won the draw.

But there was another reason why the canny Imlach dispatched this core of veteran warriors to the ice for this moment. A strict disciplinarian, many said tyrant, Imlach was also fiercely loyal to those of his subjects who sweated and sacrificed the most for the longest period of time. His end-of-game gesture on that fateful day in Maple Leaf Gardens did not go unnoticed. "I know why he put us out there. He had a group of old-timers in there, who performed greatly for him, and this was getting to be a crucial time, here in 1967. We were getting up there in age ... so he gave us a chance," said Stanley.

Imlach was the mastermind behind the Leafs' resurgence in the late 1950s and 1960s. Even players for whom he often made life a living hell, including Hall-of-Famer Frank Mahovlich, later praised the balding taskmaster's accomplishments. Mahovlich was the Maple Leafs' biggest and brightest star in terms of raw talent when Imlach arrived. But Imlach thought he wasn't tough enough, emotionally or physically, and wasn't working hard enough on the ice. With the perspective of 37 years, Mahovlich understands how

The Centennial Leafs: 1967

Imlach contributed to the success of the Maple Leafs in the 1960s. "When Punch joined the management team, he did great things. He brought in the right players. He really built that team up. He was a great leader," Mahovlich recalled. "He brought in guys that other teams didn't want. Allan Stanley had been with three teams (Boston, New York, and Chicago) prior to coming to us, and they all thought he was done. But Allan was a stalwart for us. Playing against guys like Gordie Howe, he stood up very well and proved himself time and again over the next 10 years."

A minor pro player who never really had the on-ice tools, Imlach began his coaching career in his late 20s, in the Quebec Senior League. Imlach was then recruited by the Boston Bruins organization to coach and manage their American Hockey League affiliate, the Springfield Indians.

By the late 1950s, Leafs owner, founder, and spiritual leader Conn Smythe had been looking to shake up a moribund Maple Leafs squad that had some young talent and some veterans who no longer seemed to be producing. The team hadn't won a Stanley Cup since 1951, so Smythe figured that an attitude adjustment was in order. Head coach Billy Reay was fired after a couple of lacklustre months and replaced by Imlach in November of 1958.

Imlach wanted to create a Maple Leafs team in his own image — tough and abrasive. But he also wanted a team that played like a team. Those who thought more highly of their individual skills than he felt was warranted soon found

Toronto Maple Leafs

Punch Imlach

themselves in the doghouse, or worse, on a train to the minor leagues. The formula worked, as the Leafs unexpectedly made the playoffs in Imlach's first season in charge, 1958-59. They had some ups and downs over the next couple of years, as Imlach continued to tinker with his roster, bringing in players such as Stanley, Eddie Litzenberger, and Johnny Bower. The players who had been there since before Imlach took the helm, such as Dave Keon, Tim Horton, and

The Centennial Leafs: 1967

Bob Pulford, found they liked the disciplined, hard-working approach of Imlach. Most of all, they liked the positive results it engendered. Younger players like Jim Pappin, Billy Harris, Carl Brewer, and Bob Baun also began to contribute to a team on the rise.

The Maple Leafs became a powerhouse in the first half of the 1960s, winning Stanley Cups in 1962, 1963, and 1964. Imlach continued to adjust his player personnel. He brought in Rangers star Andy Bathgate for a couple of seasons. Then, from the hockey scrap heap in 1964, he picked up goaltender Terry Sawchuk to create one of the greatest one-two punches between the pipes in hockey history — Bower and Sawchuk. The wily manager relied on veterans who would listen to him and do what he told them. But he also realized that an old team needed fresh legs. Throughout his tenure, he would inject the roster with younger players, including Ron Ellis, Brian Conacher (Charlie's son), Mike Walton, Pappin, and Peter Stemkowski.

Imlach had his detractors. By the time of the 1967 NHL expansion, his methods and attitudes were starting to seem out of touch. He never could communicate well with the new breed of wealthier, more independently-minded NHL players. Wayne Carleton, a star with the Toronto Marlboros junior team in the mid-1960s, was in Imlach's doghouse from the moment he turned pro because of his admitted bull-headedness. He argued that Imlach's rigidity foreshadowed the Leafs' downfall in the years after 1967. "He couldn't relate, either, to young people. He was used to ruling with an iron fist. Don't ask any questions. Do what you were told — the old army discipline thing." said Carleton.

But there was no doubt that Punch Imlach could squeeze more out of the agglomeration of players in 1966-67, and for most of the decade, than any coach could. "He got a lot of mileage out of players that other teams had sort of given up on. Even though these men are all honoured members of the Hockey Hall of Fame today, a big part of that is the careers they had in Toronto," said Ron Ellis. "Punch had a knack of knowing that a guy, if he was put into the right environment, could still be productive. And I think Stanley and Kelly are two good examples of that. Even [Johnny] Bower is a good example of that. Punch Imlach was a great motivator and certainly loyal."

The 1966-67 season was not all sweetness and light for the Toronto Maple Leafs. After getting off to a pretty good start, the team hit the wall. They lost 10 in a row at one stretch in the month of January. At the same time, Imlach suffered increasingly from stress and his health deteriorated. In mid-February, he was ordered by team doctors to take some time off and rest in the hospital. He was also forbidden from watching the Leafs games on TV or listening to them on the radio.

The team was slumping. The preeminent motivator in the league was having trouble motivating his charges. The wisdom of compiling such a gaggle of old-timers on one

The Centennial Leafs: 1967

roster was questioned: might they all hit the proverbial wall at the same time? So what was the tonic? It took the form of a sprightly little man with an impish grin and the charm of a leprechaun by the name of Francis "King" Clancy. A pal of team owner Conn Smythe's for more than 35 years, Clancy had been a star player with the Leafs in the late 1920s and 1930s. He had been a part of the organization — in whatever capacity Smythe wanted him — for three decades. A stark contrast to Imlach's dour dictatorship, Clancy's optimistic style was infectious. "There wasn't anybody who didn't like Clancy ... a good happy Irishman. He just came in the dressing room and was full of fire all the time," said Allan Stanley. "We got to like playing the game again with Clancy there. And that turned us right around and we went on from there."

The Leafs lost only one of their next ten games, winning seven of them under Clancy's inspiration. It was the turnaround the team needed. Showing a new resolve in Imlach's first game back, the rejuvenated Maple Leafs hammered the top-ranked Blackhawks 9-3. The league was alerted: the Maple Leafs may be old men, but under a healthy Imlach and assisted by Clancy, they were old men to contend with. The assemblage of Leafs players that had to square off against the powerful Chicago Blackhawks in the opening round of the playoffs in 1967 knew they were not favoured to win. "Chicago had Bobby Hull and Stan Mikita and Glenn Hall, Pierre Pilote. There were a lot of players on that club who were good. We knew we had our work cut out for us, and we knew who was playing and what we had to do to stop them," said Red Kelly.

Bobby Hull was one of the dominant players in the game, the second player after Maurice Richard to notch 50 goals in a season, and one of strongest players in the league. While they did not keep him off the score sheet completely, the Toronto team played solid defence. Ron Ellis, who was in his third full season in the league, recalled: "We just had superb goaltending ... Terry Sawchuk just made up his mind to come out and challenge Hull. During the regular season, he may have given Hull a little more room, but in this series, he came out and just took the angles away. And he was black and blue all over because he took those shots. Terry Sawchuk wore a belly pad that was composed of one layer of felt. That's all he had."

By now dubbed the "Over-the-Hill Gang," both as a term of endearment and mockery, the Leafs of 1967 expected even more trouble from Montreal, after it had successfully shut down Chicago. Montreal had Jean Beliveau, one of the most skillful players in the game. There was also Rocket Richard's little brother, Henri, by now a veteran superstar in his own right. The Habs were also blessed with the pugnacious combination of the goal-scoring and face-altering power of John Ferguson and the interesting goaltending tandem of Gump Worsley and the young Rogie Vachon.

In the final series, the Leafs alternated between looking ordinary, slow, and erratic and looking poised and brilliant.

The Centennial Leafs: 1967

They won games they shouldn't have, on visiting ice, and lost ones they should have, on home ice. Nonetheless, it was Toronto that held the hammer in their own barn by the time May 2 rolled around. And the role the two men in the big leather pads played in the season, the series, and the Stanley Cup win, was pivotal.

Johnny Bower was 42 years old, a cherubic, almost grandfatherly figure. The "China Wall" was affable, fun-loving, but tough as nails once he donned the pads and took his place, bare faced, in the net. Sawchuk was also competitive but had developed the contrasting reputation as a moody loner. Many felt both he and Bower were too old and no longer effective at stopping the puck and that Imlach was taking a risk icing the two geezers in 1964. When the Leafs failed to advance in the playoffs in 1965 and 1966, losing to Montreal both times, it seemed the prognostications were true. But Imlach stuck by his old-time netminders. "Imlach never gave up on Sawchuk. There weren't many teams that wanted him and he filled in great when he came to us," said Mahovlich.

Nursing a host of nagging aches and pains, Sawchuk had to come in during the middle of the Montreal series after Bower was hurt in practice one day. According to defenceman Larry Hillman, Sawchuk "flipped and flopped and he got the job done. He just went on momentum and adrenaline. Here was a chance for him to win another Cup and go out a winner."

In front of the goal, the top tandem on the Leafs

Toronto Maple Leafs

blueline, Allan Stanley and Tim Horton, played like peas in a pod, their games complementing each others'. Stanley was the stay-at-home man, doing much of the grunt work in front of the net. He stood on guard in case there was a turnover and an odd-man rush coming back towards the Toronto goal. Like Barilko, Horton's legend has grown over the years (due to his premature death in a single-vehicle car crash in 1974 and the remarkable growth of the coffee and donut empire that bears his name). What also links Barilko and Horton is the fact that they were important cogs in multiple Stanley Cup-winning hockey machines.

Horton became a regular on the Maple Leafs blueline in 1952, the year after Barilko's death. He was a seasoned veteran by the time Imlach took over the team in 1958 and was considered indispensable in the team's Cup wins in the 1960s. Known for his strength, skating ability, and physical but clean play as a teenager, Miles Gilbert (Tim) Horton hailed from eastern Ontario. He had the physique of a Greek god, and was one of the strongest and fittest athletes of his era. According to teammates, he was also a darned nice fellow and a great man to have in the dressing room.

Horton had been on the ice, not too far from Sawchuk's crease, when his long-time pal and defence partner, Stanley, stepped into the face-off circle on May 2, 1967. Horton would only last three more seasons in a Leafs uniform before moving on to New York. The rest of the vets on the ice for this historic play would not be around much longer either. Sawchuk

The Centennial Leafs: 1967

was snapped up by the Los Angeles Kings in the expansion draft over the summer of 1967. Bob Pulford would end up on the west coast with the Kings before the start of the 1970-71 season. A third member of the greying sextet who lined up for that era-ending draw, Red Kelly, would retire after the game. Coincidentally, he would also end up in L.A. — as the expansion franchise's first head coach.

As the 1960s became the 1970s, even the venerable old Johnny Bower seemed to be a relic from a different era. Relegated to a back-up role, he finally decided the rigours of hockey was no place for a man 46 years old. He retired from the game to become Toronto's goaltending coach in 1969. Of the six members of Imlach's geriatric brigade, George Armstrong would stay on the longest in the blue and white, retiring in 1971.

That same season, a shy, quiet, curly-haired 20-year-old from Kitchener made his debut for the Toronto Maple Leafs. While Darryl Sittler had a solid impact over his first few seasons, the team itself was floundering in a shallow sea of mediocrity for the first half of the 1970s. The team's fortunes, and those of their future captain, turned sharply around in the 1975-76 season. One game in particular seemed to signal the ascendancy of a future hockey superstar and also the re-emergence of a slumping dynasty.

Chapter 4
So Close and Yet So Far: 1970s

As the second intermission wound down, the score was already 8-4 in favour of the hometown Leafs. In spite of the comfortable lead, there was an unusual amount of hustle amongst the fans clamouring to get back to their seats. No one wanted to miss a moment of the action. Every time the captain's skates touched the ice — on a line change or to take a face-off — a palpable sense of anticipation gripped the fans. More than 15,000 had jammed into Maple Leaf Gardens on February 7, 1976. They were seeing action that could be immortalized in the NHL record books for decades to come.

What the Leafs fans were witnessing was more than a regular season game against a team that had been a

So Close and Yet So Far: 1970s

perennial rival since the 1920s — the Boston Bruins. The Leafs current captain, 26-year-old Darryl Sittler, was dancing his way through the Boston lineup, making a mockery of the score sheet. He had already notched three goals and four assists and was itching for more.

Halfway into the third period, the crowd was on its feet, loud and boisterous. The television camera operators were having trouble keeping their contraptions from shuddering and viewers at home felt as if they were witnessing an earthquake. Sittler was on the ice again with linemates Lanny McDonald and Errol Thompson. Days earlier, the outspoken Maple Leafs owner, Harold Ballard, had publicly challenged his superstar captain. He intimated that he might not be the right centreman for the dynamic winger duo of McDonald and Thompson. What Darryl Sittler did, on that crisp February night at the 9:27 mark, made the rotund septuagenarian eat his words. It also signaled to hockey fans that Darryl Sittler and his teammates on the Toronto Maple Leafs were a force to be reckoned with — for the first time in almost a decade.

Near the end of a shift, Thompson knew that his line was about to head off, so he flipped the puck to Sittler. Sittler had every intention of just shooting the puck into the Bruins zone before peeling back to the Leafs bench. "The funny thing was, though, as I carried the puck into the zone and I began to fade to the left, trying to get as good an angle on the net as I could, the two defencemen played me very soft. These weren't rookies, they were Dallas Smith and Gary Doak, two veterans. Dallas was playing left defence, and for some reason he seemed to get tangled up in his skates on a cross-over. At the same instant, Doak cut way over to his right. It was like a parting of the Red Sea; suddenly they just separated in front of me," Sittler said.

And, like Moses in the Old Testament, Darryl Sittler knew when something other than blind luck was working on his behalf. He took advantage of the opportunity. It was not a brilliant play, but a simple one, orchestrated by an experienced goal scorer who seemed to do no wrong on this night. "Rather than bursting through for a break-in on net, I shot back to the near post while moving to the left. [Boston goalie] Dave Reece was moving out too quickly, no doubt panicked by the sight of two veteran defenders disappearing before his eyes, and the puck dipped inside the far corner."

Sittler had not just scored another goal, but also his ninth point, breaking the record for most points in a regulation game by a single player in NHL history. The old record had been set in 1944 by Maurice Richard. When the puck went in the net, it was Sittler's fifth goal of the game. Later in the game, he found himself parked behind the Boston goal after receiving a bank pass off the boards from Lanny McDonald. Sittler threw it in front of the goal, hoping to hit the stick of an onrushing Thompson. Instead — illustrating just how much fortune was directing the proceedings this

So Close and Yet So Far: 1970s

night — the puck banked off the skate of defenceman Brad Park, and rolled over the goal line between the legs of a shell-shocked Reece.

Ten points in one game. The sheer enormity of Sittler's accomplishment is even more remarkable when you consider that the record has stood the test of time, throughout the high-scoring 1980s and early 1990s. Even as Wayne Gretzky, Mario Lemieux, Brett Hull, and Mike Gartner drove up stats as never before.

Sittler was the first, and possibly the best, of the six stars that would anchor the Maple Leafs of the 1970s. Growing up as one of eight kids in a small town in southwestern Ontario, the young Sittler got his first pair of skates from a Maple Leaf he would eventually play alongside — Rod Seiling. Seiling was winding down a most respectable NHL career, just as Sittler was on the ascent to hockey stardom.

A well-regarded player with the London Nationals (later the Knights) of the Ontario Major Junior Hockey League, Sittler had been scouted by the Maple Leafs organization and was their top pick in the 1970 amateur draft. He had 42 goals and 48 assists in his final year of junior hockey, so was expected to make a serious impact on a Maple Leafs roster looking for an identity. He was also a soft-spoken, respectful young man, according to veteran Ron Ellis. "I was impressed from day one, no question about it. This was a young guy who came in, he knew his place, and that's always a very good sign. He was

Toronto Maple Leafs

Darryl Sittler

there to listen and ask questions and learn. I was impressed with his work ethic. Darryl would be the first to admit that he didn't have the gifts of some of the other superstars, but nobody had a bigger heart, or a greater work ethic, than Darryl Sittler."

As his on-ice play improved and he became a top player in the league, Sittler's leadership skills were also coming to the

So Close and Yet So Far: 1970s

fore. Shortly after being named captain of the team in 1975, the 25-year-old also began to show the sort of independent streak that categorized the new breed of NHL player in the 1970s. Ballard had rudely dumped Sittler's mentors — former captain and legendary Leaf Dave Keon, and another fine player and true gentleman of the sport, Norm Ullman. Sittler not only objected to the moves, but to the disrespect Ballard had shown them on their way out. "These are guys who had done a lot for the Toronto club. I thought they deserved more consideration," he said at the time.

Sittler's words must have raised the hackles of Ballard, and were something the power-hungry curmudgeon would file away for future reference. But, in appreciation of his 10-point night in 1976, Ballard orchestrated an impressive pre-game ceremony. He presented his captain (posed alongside his wife Wendy and their children) with a silver tea service valued at $8,000 — an impressive amount for the era. Also standing near his best pal on that night, with a tear in his eye, was another one of the most popular Maple Leafs ever — Lanny McDonald.

Much was expected of Lanny McDonald after his stellar junior career in the Western Hockey League as a fresh-faced, somewhat nervous-looking rookie from Hanna, Alberta. McDonald, who would later score 66 goals in an NHL season with the Calgary Flames, scored only 30 during his first two NHL seasons combined. He was nearly written off. If it wasn't for a road trip early in the 1975-76 season, when he began scoring at a superstar clip, he might have been traded to the Flames while they were still in Atlanta.

On that fateful trip, coach Red Kelly (the Hockey Hall-of-Famer who won four of his eight Stanley Cups as a Maple Leafs forward) decided to replace Ellis with Sittler at centre beside McDonald. He then added another fellow who seemed to be struggling to find his game — Errol Thompson. Instant magic: the forward combination gave the Bruins fits on the record-breaking February night in 1976. That whole season, and the opportunity to room and play together in the inaugural Canada Cup tournament of 1976, solidified the friendship between the curly-tressed Sittler and the soon-to-be furry-lipped McDonald. "I think we have an unspoken faith in each other. Lanny McDonald is a truly genuine guy, down-to-earth, sincere, a character with a big heart," Sittler wrote later. And the feeling was mutual. McDonald described Sittler as, "my centre for five seasons, but more than that, my best friend."

Dave Williams, better known as "Tiger," became the dynamic duo's teammate in 1974 and their linemate in 1977. He quickly saw what made these two players so successful both on and off the ice. Like McDonald, he said, "Sittler was a class player and a good man; he always showed character on and off the ice, sometimes under the heaviest of pressure. He was a household name, but he never took anything for granted, nor the people around him."

Williams felt their line was one of the most complete

So Close and Yet So Far: 1970s

and potentially dangerous lines in the NHL. "McDonald could shoot the puck like a rocket. Sittler could do everything in a way that was well above average. And I could knock 'em down and drag 'em out." Williams was best known for his colourful personality, stick-riding antics after goals, and his fighting. But he was a hard-working player who could score as well as scrap. He was also one of the little group of forwards that was beginning to raise the hopes of Maple Leafs fans from coast to coast. He became another cog in the machinery that was being assembled to challenge the Canadiens, Bruins, Flyers, and other elite teams in the NHL.

With any contending team, the men who patrolled the blueline, keeping goals out, were as important as those who scored them. Ian Turnbull was part of the same 1973 draft as McDonald. He quickly established himself as not only one of the most effective Maple Leaf blueliners, but also one of the most enigmatic personalities to ever wear the uniform. Even some of his teammates couldn't figure out a guy who didn't seem to work at his craft, or care about squeezing the utmost out of his enormous talent. Turnbull could be the best player on the ice for a few games, and then disappear for a few more.

Another one of the sextet of stars making his debut that 1973-74 season was a gaunt-looking Swede, Borje Salming. He would prove his mettle as one of the most spellbinding, and toughest, competitors of the 1970s. He had been scouted and signed by Leafs officials watching Team Canada's exhibition games prior to the 1972 Summit Series in Moscow. While the rest of the Swedish all-stars had great skills, they seemed to lack the fire, determination, and grit needed to make it in the rough-and-tumble NHL. Salming was different. Against Team Canada, he showed a fearlessness that impressed many Canadians. Ron Ellis remembers telling Maple Leafs teammates, and anyone else who would listen, that he thought the team had a real winner in Salming. He was indeed a winner — for 17 NHL campaigns.

Tiger Williams also admired Salming from the beginning. Especially after he heard how Salming had manhandled Flyer Dave "The Hammer" Schultz when the goon, and the rest of the Broad Street Bullies of the mid-1970s, tried to intimidate the Swedish star. Tiger also liked the way Salming would save his best for when it mattered most. "Salming was a pleasure to play alongside ... an innovator, a battler and he would do as well for you under pressure in your own end as on the power play. It was reassuring just watching him lace up the skates," said Williams. When Salming picked up the puck behind his own net and dipsy-doodled through an entire team, he lifted Maple Leaf Gardens patrons out of their seats. In their excitement, they regularly knocked over the containers of stale popcorn, cold hot dogs, and flat pop that were also hallmarks of the Ballard era. Players who had a hot shot from the point were a dime a dozen. A blueliner who could turn an opposing coach's face red with rage, the opposing general manager's face green with envy, and the opposing

So Close and Yet So Far: 1970s

player's faces white with fear of potential embarrassment, was a keeper. Through the tumultuous second Imlach era, and through much of the maligned 1980s, Borje Salming was one of the few players emblazoned with a Maple Leaf worth paying money to see.

In goal seemed to be where many of the Toronto teams of the 1970s faltered. Then along came a little guy from southern Ontario, who had made his name — not to mention highlight-reel quality acrobatic saves — in the junior and minor pro ranks. Mike Palmateer planned to play the role that Chabot, Broda, and Bower had for previous Leafs champions. Like Mighty Mouse, the diminutive netminder with the big ego announced that he had come to save the day. Even after playing in the minor leagues for two seasons, he still retained the self-assuredness and showmanship that marked his successful junior days. "Palmy had the reputation of being cocky ... but he was one of those guys his teammates loved," said Sittler of the 22-year-old. Palmateer also became known as the Popcorn Kid because of his superstitious penchant for eating a small box of popcorn before every game. He taunted and frustrated opposing players. Turning routine shots on goal into dramas of Shakespearean proportions, he pumped up the Maple Leaf Gardens crowd and his teammates in the process. Hall-of-Famer Johnny Bower, who was Palmateer's goaltending coach in the late 1970s, extolled his pupil's virtues. "His reflexes are unbelievable, and I've never seen such confidence," he said.

Toronto Maple Leafs

All six of these players (Palmateer, Salming, Turnbull, Tiger, Lanny, and Sittler) had parts in the dramatic 1978 post-season. The Toronto Maple Leafs had finished the regular season with 92 points, which was 11 more than the year before. It was also the most the team had earned since 1950-51, the year Bill Barilko scored his Cup winner. Lord Stanley's Cup hadn't even been a faint hope for the Maple Leafs for a long time. All those who bled blue and white were ready for the team to make some noise in the playoffs. They wanted to show both the upstart Islanders and the confident Canadiens that the Leafs were a new team to be reckoned with.

At the time, the NHL playoffs began with a best-of-three series in the preliminary round, before the quarter finals. The Leafs found the Los Angeles Kings easy pickings, even with perennial all-star Marcel Dionne potting goals and Rogie Vachon (the goaltender who faced the Maple Leafs back in 1967 as a Canadien) keeping them out. That meant they moved on to the next round, where the New York Islanders, the third best team in the league with 111 points, were waiting. Tiger Williams said very few people outside of the Maple Leafs locker room — and only some within — were giving the team much of a shot against the Islanders.

But then a previously unheralded Leaf named Jerry Butler, a kid playing the game in as reckless and bone-jarring manner as Tiger, made his presence felt in the series. After losing the first two games on the road, Leafs coach Roger Neilson (on the advice of his favourite instigator, Tiger)

So Close and Yet So Far: 1970s

decided to change tactics to slow the New York onslaught. "In the games in Toronto, we attacked the Islanders physically and with the puck. Butler hit Bossy, who was taken off to hospital," Williams recalled proudly. "As a team, we had really got inside the Islanders, knocked them off their stride, agitated them." The tactics turned the tide.

On April 29, 1978, at the end of regulation time in game seven of the series, the score was tied 1-1. The Leafs and the Islanders then came onto the ice for the first overtime period. The prize was the chance to go head to head in the semi-finals with the two-time defending Cup champions, the Montreal Canadiens.

As blueliner Ian Turnbull was coming slowly up the left side of the ice, just outside his own blueline, he spotted Lanny McDonald racing up the right side of the ice. McDonald made an angular move into the centre of the rink near the Islanders blueline, where Turnbull hit him with a high pass that he had to knock down with his glove. "The puck kept bouncing," said McDonald. "There were three players around me all close enough to make the play, but each was thinking the other guy was going to make it. Having three guys there was probably the best thing that could have happened, because had there been only one, he would have taken me. Goalie Chico Resch came charging out of the net and I let the shot go."

McDonald became the overtime hero who scored while wearing a shield to protect his swollen broken nose and while unable to let loose one of the best wristers of the day — he had broken a bone in his wrist, too. Maybe it was because Resch was expecting one of Lanny's patented shots that he came out so far, and was caught flat footed when the flutterball came towards him. Regardless, the Toronto Maple Leafs had upset the favoured team from Long Island. Though they were swept by Montreal in four straight games in the next series, the future seemed very bright for the Leafs.

A little over a year later, the overtime hero, and one of the most talented players to ever don the blue and white, Lanny McDonald was playing in Colorado with the woeful Rockies. Two-year coach Roger Neilson, considered to be the most forward-thinking coach at the time, was no longer working for the Leafs. Neither was 10-year general manager Jim Gregory.

In December 1979, Sittler had asked that the 'C' be removed from his sweater in protest over the way Ballard and a resurrected Punch Imlach were destroying a fine organization — but mostly over the trading of McDonald. For the captain of one of the most storied teams in the league to be so confrontational was a big deal. Ballard told sportswriter Earl McRae that Sittler was little more than a traitor. "As soon as a deal can be made, his ass is gone, he said. Sittler was shipped out in early 1982.

After the surprising playoff run in 1978, Ballard's dream of finally bringing home a Stanley Cup under his stewardship had seemed within sight. But the team played only three games above .500 during the next regular season, and was

So Close and Yet So Far: 1970s

swept in the second round of the playoffs. Neilson was out, and a bald head from the past took up residence once again in the manager's office at Maple Leaf Gardens. The heartbreaking dismantling of a nearly-great team had begun. Leafs fans could only hang their heads and watch.

If not for a couple of record-breaking goal-scoring escapades and the emergence of a young scrapper from small-town Saskatchewan, the decade of the 1980s would not even be worth writing about.

Chapter 5
The Ugly Years: 1980s

The eyes of all the players on the ice were directed at the St. Louis goal or, more precisely, at the back of the St. Louis goal. The crowd in Maple Leaf Gardens had been waiting all night for this moment. Not since the night in February 1976, six years previously, when former captain Darryl Sittler scored six goals and four assists, had the Gardens witnessed the breaking of a major record. For Maple Leafs fans, it was something good to shout about — for a change.

On this evening, March 24, 1982, there were fewer suits and furs in the stands. Had he been alive, Conn Smythe would have probably argued that the evident slackening of the dress code was emblematic of a slack attitude on and off

The Ugly Years: 1980s

the ice for this current crop of young Leafs. The crowd held a lot of younger fans, too, even in the expensive gold seats close to ice level. The days of the hippies and the punks were long gone, replaced by the era of the yuppie. The 1980s were materialistic times. Slogans such as "He Who Dies With The Most Toys Wins" dominated the popular imagination.

Fans were watching the new era Toronto Maple Leafs team — with the new attitude and confidence of youth epitomized in the top forward line. Rick Vaive and Bill Derlago, along with their left winger John Anderson, made up one of the most explosive trios in the NHL. They were certainly the go-to line on the Maple Leafs of the early 1980s. There was an unspoken communication between all three men, a feel for where one another was on the ice almost all the time, and a resolute trust that their comrade would make the right play at the right time. When the trio were playing their best, which they had been for much of the past two seasons, they were nearly unstoppable.

Late in the first period of this game, the Leafs were on the power play, applying a great deal of pressure on the Blues. Bill Derlago, the flashy, talented centreman, had just embarrassed a couple of St. Louis defenders, deftly deking around them. Bruiser Dan Maloney tied up a couple more at the top of the left face-off circle. Derlago looked as though he was going to fire a shot at the rock-steady Blues netminder, Mike Liut, but saw his linemate storming towards the right side of the net out of the corner of his eye. In the split second

Toronto Maple Leafs

that makes the difference between a good playmaker and an average playmaker, Derlago slid a quick, firm backhanded pass towards the spot where he knew Rick Vaive would soon be. And he was neither disappointed nor surprised with the result.

As the lone man back, former star Canadiens defenceman Guy Lapointe handled the play as best he could. Good hockey strategy told him to take the onrushing forward when a two-on-one was closing in. Allow the goaltender to take the shooter. The theory was that the goaltender should be able to stop most shots that he could get a clear look at. Lapointe, who had come over to St. Louis a couple weeks prior to this game, couldn't contain Derlago's pass. He still slid across the ice to get a piece of Vaive's redirected shot. By the positioning of his right skate, about three inches behind the blade of Vaive's stick, he was a little too late. The Maple Leafs right winger's stick was only about six inches off the ground. It was all that one of the quickest and hardest shots in the league needed to beat goaltender Liut.

The goalie was doing what he was supposed to do as well, watching Derlago. Liut had to trust that his blueliner would take the other man and eliminate the potential for a pass. But Lapointe was new to the Blues, and still a little unfamiliar with their systems. He was also in the latter stages of an illustrious career and his reflexes were probably slower. The goal was scored.

On this fine March evening in Maple Leaf Gardens,

The Ugly Years: 1980s

this was more than just a pretty goal by an offensively gifted trio. This was history — a "first" for the Toronto Maple Leafs. Forty-eight goals had been the record for the team, set in 1960-61 by Frank Mahovlich. Neither Lanny McDonald, who scored 47 and 46 while with the Leafs, nor Darryl Sittler, who never scored more than 45, came close to beating it.

Rick Vaive had broken the magic 50 barrier. It was cruel irony that this moment would happen in an era that most Maple Leafs fans would rather forget. The 1980s were not a good time to be a Leafs fan. Richard Claude Vaive personified much that was good, and bad, about the Leafs organization during this disjointed decade. Immensely gifted as a skater, shooter, and bodychecker, he sorely lacked experience and maturity. Nonetheless, he became the youngest-ever captain, thanks to an increasingly erratic Harold Ballard's disdain for the previous bearer of the 'C', Darryl Sittler. A mere two and a half months before his record-breaking goal, Vaive had had the heavy mantle of Maple Leafs leadership thrust upon his somewhat bewildered shoulders. He was just 22 years of age.

Vaive was the classic case of a young man given too much, too soon. His wisdom took many years to catch up to his talent. Like the team he led, Vaive showed flashes of brilliance, but also great moments of recklessness and undisciplined play. Expected to lead the Toronto Maple Leafs out of the wilderness, he had to do so with a weak supporting cast. He had great linemates in Anderson and Derlago, but one good line does not a team make. Throughout most of the

Toronto Maple Leafs

1980s, the Maple Leafs forwards were pretty good at scoring goals, while the defencemen occasionally stopped opposing players from doing the same. Once in a while, one of the cast of cast-offs who tended net for Toronto managed to save a game with a save. The few veterans on the roster were either indifferent or rapidly losing whatever skills they may have once had. The teams that were iced for most of the decade were a far cry from the team that upset the Islanders in the 1978 playoffs.

Only Borje Salming was left from the old guard when Vaive popped his 50th goal. After cleaning house in 1979, Ballard had forced general manager Jim Gregory to start making changes when his team started to falter. For next to nothing, promising young blueliner Randy Carlyle was traded, along with solid centreman George Ferguson. Carlyle would go on to win a Norris Trophy, playing in the NHL for another 16 seasons. Hard-hitting players Brian Glennie and Jack Valiquette, because they were pals of the Sittler-McDonald-Williams cabal, were dealt away. So were Trevor Johansen and Don Ashby.

After Imlach took over as the Leafs' general manager from the fired Gregory, the Toronto Maple Leafs got a dose of some old-time hockey religion. Imlach sent Lanny McDonald to Colorado because he felt it was the best way to break up what he called the "county-club atmosphere" that Sittler and his cronies had created at Maple Leaf Gardens. Even after Imlach was shoved aside by Ballard in 1981, the process

The Ugly Years: 1980s

he had started continued unabated, with Sittler eventually leaving Toronto. He was dealt to the Philadelphia Flyers for a player named Rich Costello and a second-round draft choice. The Leafs also dumped top defender Ian Turnbull and netminder Mike Palmateer, with little to show in return. The six players who defined an entire generation of Maple Leafs hockey — McDonald, Sittler, Turnbull, Palmateer, Williams, and Salming — were reduced to a rump of one. The only deal which most hockey observers say was a moderately good one for the team was the one that sent journeymen Jerry Butler and Tiger Williams to Vancouver for a couple of hot young guns, Rick Vaive and Bill Derlago in February 1980.

Vaive was born in the nation's capital, but spent much of his youth in Canada's smallest province, Prince Edward Island, where he went to high school and played provincial Junior A. In two seasons of major junior hockey with Sherbrooke, Vaive lit the lamp 127 times, adding 138 assists for a whopping 265 points. The hard-shooting winger came to the attention of scouts across North America. The NHL was still the top league. Its chief competitor for talent, the World Hockey Association, was in its death throes with its remaining franchises desperately negotiating their entryway into the NHL. But there was still great competition for young hockey talent between the two leagues.

Nineteen-year-old Rick Vaive was already playing professional hockey for the Birmingham Bulls of the WHA when he was drafted by the Vancouver Canucks in the first round, fifth overall, in the 1979 NHL entry draft. The WHA folded after the 1978-79 season. Only the Edmonton Oilers, Winnipeg Jets, Quebec Nordiques, and Hartford Whalers were invited to join the NHL. The Bulls dissolved, its players going to whichever NHL franchise held their rights, which meant the Canucks for Vaive.

When he came to Vancouver, Vaive was expected to continue the goal-scoring exploits of his youth, which included a decent 26-goal performance with the Bulls. He didn't dazzle out of the chute, notching only 13 goals in 47 games. He was also expected to be physical and disciplined, on and off the ice. When the Canucks had a chance to improve their club by acquiring the veteran experience and grit of Dave "Tiger" Williams and Jerry Butler, they sacrificed an underachieving pair of young forwards. Vaive and Derlago became members of the Toronto Maple Leafs.

Derlago had been no slouch as a junior player either. Born in the small town of Birtle, Manitoba, the star with the Brandon Wheat Kings of the Western Hockey League had compiled statistics that made Vaive's seem ordinary by comparison. In his three seasons of junior, he had goal totals of 48, 96, and 89.

Both players more or less welcomed the trade to Toronto, as it meant a chance to strut their offensive stuff. The Canucks hadn't appreciated Vaive — they thought he had a bad attitude and drank too much. Their former coach, Harry Neale, felt both Derlago and Vaive lacked the work

The Ugly Years: 1980s

ethic and maturity necessary to play for a contending team. He thought they were on the Vancouver Canucks roster at the wrong time.

Leaf Terry Martin was, by contrast, certainly impressed with new teammate, Vaive. "He had a great shot off the wing. And it would either go just inside the post or he would overpower the goaltender with the puck hitting the pad and it trickling through the legs," Martin said. "But he also took a beating in front of the net to score goals."

And Vaive did score lots of goals in Toronto. Even though early in the year, he had only seven or eight goals, he then had five consecutive two-goal games. He went from eight goals to about 18 in a matter of just over two weeks. Derlago explained why: "In Toronto, we had a lot of ice time, which was key. And we were sort of just free-wheeling, playing like we did in junior. We had fun," he said. "We didn't win many games, but we scored some goals. There were a lot of 6-5 games, and that's when Gretzky was around and ... it was sort of end-to-end hockey, with the last shot winning. We would hang in there for a couple of periods, but then the lack of experience would kill us."

The lack of experience came as a result of Imlach first alienating, then trading most of it away in his short return appearance. Maybe, if Don Cherry hadn't been such a man of his word, perhaps the whole debacle of the 1980s would never have happened.

Before bringing back Imlach, Harold Ballard had

Toronto Maple Leafs

considered both Scotty Bowman and Don Cherry as the new coach for the Leafs. Bowman politely declined. The one guy Ballard liked who liked him back — Cherry — had already begun negotiations to be the head coach of the sad-sack Colorado Rockies. Cherry had actually made a verbal agreement, so when Ballard made his formal offer, Cherry said he was sorry, but he had to refuse it.

It didn't take long after Imlach was hired in July, 1979, for Ballard to get the first twinge of regret. Imlach, whose career had peaked when many of his new players were in peewee hockey, still believed that the methods that worked on the Allan Stanleys, George Armstrongs, and Tim Hortons of the world, could work on the Salmings, Sittlers, McDonalds, and Palmateers. The family that had been created in the latter part of the 1970s was ripped apart without positive effects on the team's showing on the ice. When Punch began suffering heart problems again in 1981, Ballard removed him from his position of general manager. He replaced him with the first available friendly face he saw — scout Gerry McNamara.

However, in addition to Ballard's boorish behaviour, and his poor choices for coach and general manager in the 1980s, he was cheap. McNamara was given only a bare-bones scouting staff. He did not have the resources to properly look at all of junior hockey and the minor pro ranks, let alone do any extensive European scouting. As the Leafs dropped in the standings, year by year, their choices in the first-round of the draft went higher and higher. But McNamara had little to

The Ugly Years: 1980s

work with on draft day, and often had to go with his gut when making his call from the podium. This resulted in a rash of bad draft choices. Players who were properly studied and scouted could have had their deficiencies laid bare before draft day, instead of after they put on a Maple Leafs uniform.

The only time McNamara managed to land a big fish, it was a no-brainer. Wendel Clark was considered to be the top prospect heading into the 1985 draft. As a bruising, brawling defenceman with the Saskatoon Blades of the Western Hockey League, Clark had scored 155 points in two seasons. Harold Ballard was ecstatic when Clark was chosen. Clark seemed pretty happy, too. When he began scoring, and pounding and pummeling opponents, long-suffering Maple Leafs fans saw a new blue-and-white hero on the rise.

But coaching continued to be an area where Ballard let his fans down. Usually, the general manager decided whom he would have patrolling the bench for the team. As the team's fortunes slumped on the ice, the job of coaching the Toronto Maple Leafs was rapidly losing its lustre — thanks mostly to Ballard's interference. After watching two of Punch Imlach's protégés, Floyd Smith and Joe Crozier, fail miserably, Ballard took matters into his own hands. He hired affable former Philadelphia and New York Rangers assistant Mike Nykoluk. Imlach, surprisingly, had wanted to hire a bright young coach named Doug Carpenter. He was overruled.

The decision seemed inspired at first. The Maple Leafs showed some promise as they went 15-15-10 over

Toronto Maple Leafs

the remaining 40 games of the 1980-81 regular season. But Nykoluk was neither a good motivator of an under-talented and under-achieving squad, nor a very good bench general. The team averaged only 27 wins per season over the next three seasons.

Imlach was long-gone, replaced by the ineffectual McNamara by the time Ballard hired John Brophy to replace another coach who had bolted for a decent salary. As a player in his heyday, Brophy would have made Tiger Williams or Tie Domi look like a cream puff. The character of Reggie Dunlop (played by Paul Newman) from the movie *Slap Shot* could have been pulled from the biographical detail of Brophy's career. In nearly 20 years of bruising, bus-riding minor league hockey, Brophy had averaged more than 230 minutes in penalties per season.

But it was as a coach that he is best remembered. Brophy worked his way up and through practically every professional hockey league on the continent. Only Scotty Bowman had as many victories over his career — more than 1,000. Behind the bench, Brophy's ruddy face became redder than normal when his team was assessed a penalty or an offside was missed by an official. He was a screamer and a motivator who was able to squeeze maximum effort from minimum talent. "I remember playing in Minnesota once," recalled former Leaf Eddie Olczyk. "We were losing 4-1 after the first period. After he yelled at us and started walking out, he stopped at the door. 'You guys look like you're sound asleep out there.

The Ugly Years: 1980s

So when you're asleep at home, the lights are out.' And he turned the lights out." Players fumbled over one another as they tried to move around the darkened dressing room. Finally, veteran Borje Salming decided enough was enough, and turned the lights back on. Brophy came back, cursed Salming, and promptly turned the lights out again.

Unpopular with some players for his methods, Brophy still managed to take a talent-poor Maple Leafs team to the playoffs in his first two seasons with the club. They went to the second round in 1986-87 and lost in the first the following season. Brophy's act wore thin with many players, particularly Rick Vaive. By this time, Vaive had been stripped of his captaincy for missing a practice after a night of revelry.

As Ballard's health declined in the late 1980s, so did his club's fortunes. The turmoil behind the scenes, inside the dressing room, and in the front office of the Toronto Maple Leafs generated more press than the performance of the team on the ice. John Brophy was axed 33 games into the 1988-89 season. George Armstrong, was drafted from his duties as a scout to coach for a time. (Armstrong had been the longest serving captain in the history of the Toronto Maple Leafs and the man who scored the clinching goal in the deciding game of the 1967 Stanley Cup finals.) Tom Watt and Doug Carpenter (finally) got their turn, too, behind the bench.

The Maple Leafs organization of the day didn't seem to know how to use some of the fine young talent they did manage to draft. While there were many draft busts in the 1980s, there were also a number of good players who were pegged by Maple Leafs scouts and subsequently signed to the team. Wendel Clark was such a complete player with both hockey savvy and an inbred prairie work ethic that all a coach had to do was wind him up and let him go. Without competent coaching, veteran role models, and a winning atmosphere, however, it was hard for these players to develop properly. An impatient owner and fan base didn't help. Youngsters were often promoted up from the minors before they had gained enough pro experience: players such as Gary Nylund, Al Iafrate, Luke Richardson, and Vince Damphousse. Many players simply showed up for a few games, and when they didn't return the team to glory, they were shunted aside.

If Ballard had given up control of the team earlier in the decade, would the team have spent more money on coaching, scouting, and hockey operations staff? Would all the old Stanley Cup banners and other tangible reminders of the team's glorious past have been thrown on the rubbish heap? Would veteran Leafs greats have been shunned by the organization to which they had brought so much acclaim? All that can be said for certain is that when Harold Ballard died, the 1980s very quickly became just a bad memory.

Chapter 6
The Dougie Era: 1990s

By late in the 1992-93 NHL season, Doug Gilmour was already a household name in Canada. His record-breaking offensive season had helped the Toronto Maple Leafs complete their best regular season in nearly 45 years. "Dougie Gilmour is the best hockey player in the world today," proclaimed Don Cherry during a *Coach's Corner* episode. And for one glorious 41-day playoff period in the late spring of 1993, the statement was more than just one good ol' Kingston boy giving kudos to another.

On May 3, Gilmour and the Leafs were playing in the Norris Division final against the St. Louis Blues. The game seemed to be lasting an eternity. In the near delirium of action that had been transpiring on the ice for four full periods of playoff hockey, the temperature, emotions, and blood pressure of the 15,000 patrons inside Maple Leaf Gardens had risen steadily. The shot totals were also climbing to stratospheric heights. Toronto already had more than 60 shots on goal.

A shy but steely-eyed thief named Curtis Joseph was guarding the goal for the St. Louis Blues. Before the opening game of the series, the netminder had been known as a pretty decent, and occasionally spectacular, performer. By the time the cheering died down this particular evening, the exploits of Curtis Joseph ("Cujo") would be on the minds of all those who had watched the game. Cujo had been unthinkably brilliant all night. His reflexes were sharp, his positioning bang-on, his decisions lightning quick. He was in the zone. But even though he made an astonishing 62 saves, Cujo actually lost the game.

It took a very special, unexpected play to beat him on this night. The eminently talented, scrappy Dougie Gilmour was up to the task. Looking like the second coming of Dave Keon with some Wayne Gretzky pizzazz thrown in, the small-framed 30-year-old exuded focus and intensity, qualities for which he was renowned throughout the league.

In his minor hockey and junior days, Gilmour had apparently had to use every trick in the book to appear taller and heavier to impress scouts and coaches. The longer the season went, the smaller he appeared to get. By this point in

The Dougie Era: 1990s

the post-season, after all the pounding, up to 30 minutes of ice time per game, the hooks and the jabs, he looked positively emaciated. But after every exhausting shift — each time he picked himself off the ice after being knocked down by a larger opponent, each time he sliced and swerved through the opponent's defensive alignment with his smooth skating stride, or checked their top player into frustration — Dougie Gilmour actually seemed to be playing better.

The action had been hot and heavy at times during the first overtime period on this night. The Leafs had seen so many spectacular saves snuff out otherwise glorious scoring chances, that some may have felt that the hockey gods were aligned against them. But Dougie kept trying.

Like a certain number 99, Dougie loved to set up behind the opposition goal with the puck. A defenceman on the other team had a tough decision to make: should he chase him behind the net and hope to check him before he threw the puck out to a teammate that the defenceman was also supposed to be covering? Or should he stay in his spot and hope Dougie couldn't manage to make a precision pass to either one of his linemates, or couldn't score a wraparound goal himself? This night, on this play, Murray Baron and Rick Zombo were the two Blues defencemen who had to make that decision. Zombo decided he would keep his eyes on the blue-and-white behemoth that was sliding in and out of the slot — Dave Andreychuk. That left poor Baron to make the fateful call.

Toronto Maple Leafs

Doug Gilmour

As Andreychuk battled with Zombo on Cujo's immediate right, the talented Russian Nikolai Borschevsky stayed farther out, near the bottom of the right face-off circle. He was marked fairly closely by Kevin Miller. The throng of blue-and-white faithful was on its feet, shaking the cavernous Maple Leaf Gardens with a resounding din.

Gilmour slid around behind the goal, moving from side

The Dougie Era: 1990s

to side. He could see that both his wingers were well covered and the defencemen were a little too far away. He probably didn't want to risk a long pass that could be deflected out to no-man's land. In an instant, his years of training, hockey sense, and inspiration all came together. He dug his skates in and moved as if he were going to slip around the left side of the St. Louis goal to try a back-handed wraparound. Instead, Gilmour performed the perfect "Savardian spinarama," catching everyone off-guard. He executed it so quickly, he jammed the puck into a nearly empty right side of the goal. Cujo would have had to extend his right leg another eight inches, or bend over completely backwards, in order to have stopped the puck from going in.

The arena erupted into bedlam. The Leafs had won the game 2-1 in double overtime. Although it would take another six games for the series to be decided in Toronto's favour, the Leafs would go on to play in the Stanley Cup semi-finals for the first time since 1967. At long last, suffering Maple Leafs fans had a legitimate hope for better days ahead. The team was entertaining and very, very good. There was a professional hockey man at the helm, a coach-of-the-year behind the bench, and a fearless captain with gas left in the tank. They also had a true-to-life superstar who had led the cast of capable supporting characters through the team's most successful regular season, and their most inspiring playoff run, in three decades. And assembling these pieces had taken a little less than two years.

Toronto Maple Leafs

Harold Ballard had finally passed away in April 1990. It had still taken more than a year of backroom machinations to settle affairs at Maple Leaf Gardens. Cliff Fletcher — the recently-retired general manager of the 1989 Stanley Cup champion Calgary Flames — was recruited to run the Maple Leafs. The official announcement was finally made on June 5, 1991. The dark clouds that had been hovering over Maple Leaf Gardens for two decades suddenly parted to usher in big changes. The Gardens itself soon became a relic of a former era.

An astute constructor of teams, Fletcher had cut his teeth with the Montreal Canadiens in the late 1960s. When the expansion Atlanta Flames were looking for a young executive to take over the team's hockey operations in the early 1970s, they selected Fletcher. He continued in that job for nearly 20 years. With a mix of still-effective, hungry veterans and a few young studs, the Flames had been on even terms with their provincial rivals, the Edmonton Oilers, for much of the latter half of the decade. They won the Stanley Cup in 1989 — thanks to captain Lanny McDonald and a core of talented young players, including Doug Gilmour (whom Fletcher had picked up in 1988).

Bringing Fletcher on board was a sign that the Toronto Maple Leafs wanted the best and were now willing to pay for it. An image overhaul began with Fletcher's hiring: the Leafs created and hung new Stanley Cup banners and welcomed alumni back into the fold. Fletcher hired former captain

The Dougie Era: 1990s

Darryl Sittler as an assistant later that year. Mere weeks into the job, Fletcher also signaled a change in the on-ice product as well. From the Edmonton Oilers, he picked up future Hall-of-Famers Glenn Anderson and Grant Fuhr, both four-time Stanley Cup winners.

But the Toronto Maple Leafs were still not a very good team. After an embarrassing 12-1 loss to Mario Lemieux, Jaromir Jagr, and the rest of the Pittsburgh Penguins on December 12, 1991, Fletcher began to plan for an even bigger change. The Maple Leafs had won only 10 games by New Year's Day. One day later, the fortunes of a franchise that was already taking baby steps back towards respectability grew exponentially.

The 10-player deal consummated by Cliff Fletcher with his former Flames assistant, Doug Risebrough, must still give the understudy nightmares. The Flames received former 51-goal scorer Gary Leeman, who had been struggling since his historic performance in the 1989-90 season, bruiser Craig Berube, journeyman defender Michel Petit, young Russian hopeful Alexander Godynyuk, and netminder Jeff Reese. In return, the Leafs got three players who wanted out of Calgary because they didn't think they were getting a fair shake financially: defencemen Jamie Macoun and Ric Nattress, and Doug Gilmour. The Leafs also got goalie Rick Walmsley (who would go on to be the team's goaltending coach after retiring) as well as young forward Kent Manderville.

Gilmour welcomed the chance to get away from an

Toronto Maple Leafs

increasingly nasty contract squabble and come to one of the most celebrated franchises in sports history. One returning Maple Leafs player, Mark Osborne, had the unique perspective to compare the atmosphere around the team BD (Before Dougie) and AD (After Dougie). He returned a couple of months after the Gilmour deal. "I think the biggest difference was the level of professionalism and maturity," he said. "There's a certain aura about winning a Stanley Cup, and respect comes with that. When you look at Glenn Anderson, or Dougie Gilmour, there's that seriousness of taking their game to another level — that when the game is on, it's for keeps."

The Maple Leafs almost squeaked into the playoffs in 1992. At least they knew that the crew for the good ship Maple Leaf had been assembled for the following year's race. Cliff Fletcher simply needed the right captain at the helm. He chose an ex-undercover cop from Montreal, Pat Burns. He lured Burns away from the Montreal Canadiens, and the only job in pro hockey where coaches and players faced tougher scrutiny from the media than in Toronto.

Burns looked like a cop. Big and burly, fiercely competitive, he was a player's coach, but not a pushover. Gilmour explained, "He made a family of it. At the same time, if you didn't play well, he was all over you."

After a shaky start to the 1992-93 regular season, Pat Burns' Leafs wound up setting team records for wins (44), for most home wins (25), and for most points by the team in

The Dougie Era: 1990s

its history with 99. Gilmour did his bit, too. He set franchise records for points (127), assists (95), and most points for a centre. Borschevsky set the first-year player record for points with 74. His 34 goals tied Wendel Clark for the team record for a rookie as well.

But the Maple Leafs really began their resurgence in the playoffs. Their 99 points only meant a third-place finish in the highly-competitive Norris Division, behind Chicago and Detroit. The Chicago Blackhawks met the St. Louis Blues who had barely squeaked into the post-season with 85 points. But thanks to the magic of Curtis Joseph, the Blues upset the Hawks in only four games. The second-place Red Wings were expected to be too strong for the Maple Leafs, despite Toronto's good season. Detroit, led by Hart Trophy winner Steve Yzerman and the budding Russian superstar Sergei Fedorov, had solid goaltending in Tim Cheveldae, and an experienced blueline of Mark Howe, Brad McCrimmon, and Dino Ciccarelli.

After the Maple Leafs fell by scores of 6-3 and 6-2 in the first two games in Detroit, all pundits figured the series was over. Anyone at Maple Leaf Gardens for the next two games saw differently. The Leafs won the third game 4-2 and the fourth 3-2. Wendel Clark was back to the Clark of old. He regained the mantle as the inspirational force of the Maple Leafs team. Gilmour was able to keep Yzerman off the score sheet for the most part. Felix Potvin proved to everyone that the trading away of Grant Fuhr had not been a mistake.

Toronto Maple Leafs

Potvin had been a standout with Chicoutimi of the Quebec Major Junior Hockey League as well as during his brief stint in the minors. He became Fuhr's full-time backup early in the 1992-93 campaign, replacing the future Hall-of-Famer when he was injured or needed rest. He impressed fans, the media, and his bosses with his effective, occasionally spectacular, play. For the first time since Mike Palmateer, the Toronto Maple Leafs had a young goaltender around which a franchise could be built.

The package that saw Fuhr dealt to Buffalo, allowing Potvin to be the number one guy in goal, also included a hulking mass of scoring touch named Dave Andreychuk. While Gilmour was having pretty good success with Glenn Anderson and Borschevsky on his line, he became absolutely devastating as a set-up man once the six-foot-four-inch, 220-pound winger was grafted on to his line.

As a 10-year veteran of the Buffalo Sabres, Andreychuk had averaged 30 or so goals per season, hitting the 40-mark twice. Over the first 52 games of the 1992-93 season, he had scored a very respectable 29 goals. Paired with Gilmour after February, he notched 25 more in only 31 games, to set an all-time Maple Leafs record for goals by a player in a single season. He did nearly as well in 1993-94 with 53 tallies. He was only the second player after Rick Vaive to have back-to-back 50-goal years. Throughout his tenure with the Maple Leafs, Andreychuk used his size and incredible reach to score his goals. He was extremely difficult to move from in front of

The Dougie Era: 1990s

the goal. With great control of his long stick, he could literally wrap the puck around the entire breadth of a sprawled goalie and deposit it in the net.

The Maple Leafs needed seven games in the 1993 playoffs to defeat the Blues. All that stood between the team and a berth in the Stanley Cup finals were the Los Angeles Kings.

The Kings had made it to the Western Conference finals after defeating the Pat Quinn-led Vancouver Canucks. It was the farthest the Californian team had gone in the playoffs in its 26-year history. They had speed and skill with Tony Granato, Tomas Sandstrom, and Luc Robitaille up front, stud defencemen Rob Blake, Darryl Sydor, and Alexei Zhitnik on the blueline, and the headband-wearing goalie, Kelly Hrudey, between the pipes. They also had former Edmonton Oiler greats Jari Kurri, Marty McSorley, Charlie Huddy, and Wayne Gretzky on the roster.

The Maple Leafs had home ice advantage. The series was billed as a showdown between the Great One and Dougie Gilmour. Gilmour had idolized Gretzky as a young player, even tucking in one side of his hockey sweater à la 99. But, playing the best hockey of anyone at the time, Dougie won round one.

Round two took place on May 17, 1993, at Maple Leaf Gardens. The hometown team was again locked in a 1-1 standstill with the visitors. During the third period, the Leafs compiled a lopsided 22-1 shots-on-goal margin and scored three times. "Gilmour flipped Kings rookie Alexei Zhitnik on

Toronto Maple Leafs

his face with a textbook hip-check, set up Glenn Anderson for what proved to be the winner, scored the third Leafs' goal himself, and then created the fourth by Bill Berg with another assist," remembered one impressed sportswriter. Gilmour also registered the first goal of the game for Toronto, so he had a hand in every Maple Leafs scoring play of the night. Gilmour was so dominant that some of the Kings decided to take some cheap shots at the Leafs' star. The most vicious came when 235-pound Gretzky bodyguard Marty McSorley caught Gilmour full force with an elbow as Gilmour crossed over the L.A. blueline carrying the puck. Gilmour may have had his head down, but Marty led with the elbow. The hit was meant to send a message.

Almost immediately after the hit, Wendel Clark, who had in many respects handed over on-ice emotional and actual leadership of the Leafs to Gilmour, reminded the hockey world just why he is so beloved in Toronto. As Gilmour lay on the ice, Clark went over to "talk to Marty." He blackened the larger man's eye with a couple of round-house rights. "Well, I saw our best player lying on the ice, maybe badly hurt, so I just reacted," explained Clark after the game.

The series would be a back and forth affair that would see Clark continue to play exceedingly well, scoring a hat trick in the sixth game of the series. But a controversial non-call in that game — when Gretzky's stick clipped Gilmour in overtime — came at a bad time. The Leafs already had Glenn Anderson in the penalty box. Referee Kerry Fraser neither

The Dougie Era: 1990s

saw the play, nor questioned either of his linesmen.

So, Gretzky was spared a penalty and ended up scoring the game-winning goal shortly thereafter. The tied series went back to Toronto for the seventh game. The Great One rose to the occasion and beat Toronto 5-3. He shattered the dreams of not only Maple Leafs fans, but all Canadian hockey fans. Waiting for the winner of the series was the Montreal Canadiens. It could have been the most monumental series in the modern day NHL — the two most storied hockey franchises, Toronto and Montreal, playing each other for the Stanley Cup again. "It all happened so quickly," said Mark Osborne of the unlikely playoff run in the spring of 1993. "I mean, we played three seven-game series in 42 nights ... we started gaining some momentum. It was a special run, and it's too bad it didn't turn out the way we had hoped."

The following season, Toronto won its first 10 games in a row en route to a record of 43-29-12 for 98 points. The team was just two back of Detroit for top of the newly-named Central Division. Gilmour had another stellar season, notching 111 points. Toronto played Chicago in the first round of the playoffs. In goal for the Hawks was another player who would have an interesting future as far as the Toronto Maple Leafs were concerned — Ed Belfour. He reminded fans of Curtis Joseph and his game-saving heroics of the year before. But Potvin was the better goalie, earning three shutouts in the series as Toronto dispatched the Hawks in six games.

Next came the San Jose Sharks. They had dealt Detroit

Toronto Maple Leafs

its unexpected second-straight first-round exit. Only five years old, the Sharks franchise fought the Maple Leafs tooth and nail for a spot in the conference finals. Toronto needed a 4-2 decision in game seven to win that series. Waiting for Toronto was a rested Vancouver Canucks team, still coached by the temperamental but brilliant Pat Quinn. On paper, the Canucks didn't appear to be much better than Toronto. However, they were younger, a little faster, and a lot healthier. Many of the Maple Leafs veterans were playing hurt. Doug Gilmour was skating on a badly injured ankle.

Injuries, fatigue, and a lack of depth meant a hasty five-game exit for the Maple Leafs that season. Although fans were disappointed, they felt that with a little tweaking, some healthy bodies, and a dose of good fortune, Toronto would again take the Maple Leafs nation to another Stanley Cup victory. Cliff Fletcher was a little more concerned about the team's failings. He felt more drastic measures were needed, both for the short and long-term health of the team.

Before the decade of the 1990s was over, Fletcher would no longer be at the helm. The team would have gone through a string of coaches, panicked player acquisitions, and not one but two returns of a prodigal son named Wendel. By 1999, with a talented and tougher-than-expected Swede as captain and a Hall of Fame netminder, the old Punch Imlach strategy resurfaced. Getting the most from a bunch of over-the-hill vets, sprinkled with youthful enthusiasm, was helping the Toronto Maple Leafs return to the status of an elite

The Dougie Era: 1990s

NHL team. The recipe would also lead them into a period of unparalleled rivalry with a team that hadn't even been in existence when the 1990s started. The next chapter in the Toronto Maple Leafs' amazing story is still being written. Its plot revolves around a titanic clash between teams from the nation's capital and the centre of the hockey universe.

Chapter 7
The Battle of Ontario: 2000–4

The Toronto Maple Leafs had just about eliminated Ottawa from the Stanley Cup playoffs for the fourth time in five years, and Leaf forward Darcy Tucker was already mockingly waving goodbye to the Senators' rough and tough right winger Chris Neil. The gesture was full of symbolism, and more than a little juvenile, but will be remembered by the Senators' players, fans, and management for a long, long time.

The Maple Leafs' win in 2004 was tougher on the Senators than the rest. Things were supposed to be different this year for the talented young team from the nation's capital. And to have Tucker give the gut-wrenching, despairing exclamation mark was almost too much to bear.

The Battle of Ontario: 2000-4

At the best of times, Tucker looks like a grown-up version of one of the Little Rascals. But he can also look positively devilish when inspired. He has a habit of growing a goatee, then shaving off the mustache portion, leaving a dark, short-cropped undergrowth that matches the colour of his Spock-like eyebrows. He is a player who makes life miserable for opposing players — hacking, berating, ramming them into the end boards, sometimes all on one shift.

Coming into the NHL, first with Montreal, then moving on to Tampa Bay, Tucker often got his teams in penalty trouble when he lost his cool. He had a style of play only a fan of his team could love. But it was effective, and something Maple Leafs head coach Pat Quinn wanted when he signed him up two-thirds of the way through the 1999-2000 season. "He's a guy who plays on emotion. You always want to make sure when you have that, it's an asset, and I call it an asset with Darcy," said Quinn. "You want to hold it in check if you can. [But] it's what gives you an edge."

Emotion gets stoked higher and hotter during the regular season, becoming positively volcanic once the post-season comes around. Usually only the veteran players — and occasionally the rare younger one like Tucker — can channel this emotion into beating the opposing team. That's why Quinn seems to prefer veterans. It's why Punch Imlach preferred veterans in the 1960s. In 2004, the Toronto Maple Leafs seemed to possess that intangible veteran chutzpah that Ottawa was missing in all four of their meetings in the post season.

Toronto Maple Leafs

On April 20, 2004, the latest tilt between the provincial rivals was in its final minutes. The Toronto Maple Leafs had a 4-1 lead in this seventh game of the opening round of the Stanley Cup playoffs. The clock was approaching 10 p.m. as Tucker tangled with a few of the frustrated and dispirited Senators players, resulting in the usual pushing and shoving. If not for the linesman holding him back very firmly, Chris Neil may have thrown caution to the wind. It looked like the last game of the season for his team. He would have loved to take out his frustration on Tucker's 5-foot-10-inch, 180-pound frame. Tucker knew it, so he spent a couple of extra seconds making sure Neil and the rest of the Senators saw his exaggerated wave before being ushered off the ice. Less than a minute remained in regulation time.

The crowd at the Air Canada Centre — the Leafs' new, state-of-the-art home since 1999 — loved it. Roaring their approval for Tucker's gesture, thousands belted out the lyrics to "Na Na Hey Hey Goodbye." (The Montreal Canadiens' victory chant had been adopted by many home teams enjoying a playoff series win.) As also happened after every playoff series win since Dougie and pals defeated Detroit in 1993, Maple Leafs fans flooded the streets. They filled up local watering holes, and drove around honking their horns and flying their flags. Beating Ottawa was sweet. For an entire generation of Leafs fans who could not fathom what a Stanley Cup win would feel like, this would have to do.

Ottawa head coach Jacques Martin must have known

The Battle of Ontario: 2000-4

that Tucker's gesture meant that he too would soon be waving goodbye to his parking space at the Corel Centre. Not long after the series finale, after eight and a half seasons behind the bench, Martin was fired. Many such changes were inevitable in an organization that had a dismal rate of failure when playing one particular opponent in the post season. Martin had led the team to great regular season heights. He had helped build an exciting, energetic, and entertaining team and made it all the way to the semi-finals of the NHL post-season. But he couldn't get his charges to beat the Toronto Maple Leafs when it mattered most. The concept of one team "having the number" of another team is well-known in the annals of sport, and this was a classic case.

The 2004 series stood as an example of the sometimes illogical nature of the sport. The Ottawa Senators had led the league in goal scoring with 262 in the regular season, yet they could only score 11 in a seven-game series. In the four games they lost against Toronto, Ottawa scored a grand total of one goal — and that came in the climactic game of the series. The goal came off the stick of Tucker's counterpart on the Senators, Vaclav Varada. None of the superstars — Marian Hossa, Daniel Alfredsson, or Magnus Arvedson — managed to score goals. Nor did the Senators get the kind of offensive support from defencemen Wade Redden and Chris Phillips that they had hoped for. In some cases, their own-zone giveaways proved deadly to a pouncing Toronto forecheck.

The shots-on-goal totals for the series also told a strange

Toronto Maple Leafs

story — 238 to 154 in favour of the Senators. And these numbers were not unusual. Over the four playoff series, the vast majority of the games had lopsided shot totals favouring the Sens. In nearly every game the Senators lost, they had outshot the Maple Leafs.

For the first six games of the 2004 series, Ottawa had carried the play to the Maple Leafs, just as they had in the majority of the games in each of the three previous series. But in the seventh game, a critical juncture, the Maple Leafs seemed to rally and play their most complete game. Players finished their checks more aggressively and consistently. They played hard each and every second they were on the ice. There were fewer miscues and mental errors. The goaltending of Belfour was amazing. Toronto's youngsters like Nik Antropov and Alexei Ponikarovsky stepped up their play, following the lead of battered veterans Joe Nieuwendyk, Gary Roberts, Tie Domi, and Eddie Belfour.

Even though the Maple Leafs weren't as healthy a group as the younger Senators, they did have experience on their side. Outside the overpaid and under-producing New York Rangers, and the ancient Detroit Red Wings, there were no other teams carrying more players over 35 than the Maple Leafs. And the team got older at the trading deadline. They acquired future Hall of Fame defenceman Brian Leetch from the New York Rangers where he had played for 17 years, and 41-year-old Ron Francis who won two Stanley Cups in the early 1990s.

The Battle of Ontario: 2000-4

To be fair, there was another big factor in all four playoff series wins: the dude in the fibreglass and wire mesh mask at the Maple Leafs' end of the rink. The first three times Ottawa played against the Maple Leafs in the playoffs (2000, 2001, and 2002), Curtis Joseph was the netminder who broke the Senators' hearts. Cujo played for Toronto very much the way he had played against Toronto back in the second-round of the 1993 playoffs — brilliantly. He took more shots per game, practically every game, than his opponents' goalie. If he had a rare bad game, he would inevitably bounce back with an incredible performance the next time out. When Cujo was "on," Ottawa was in trouble.

In the 2004 campaign, it was Eddie Belfour's turn to face Ottawa. Thirty-eight-year-old Belfour from Carman, Manitoba, had joined the Leafs before the 2002-03 season. In four games, he allowed only one goal. Then, as the Senators players became faint-hearted, losing their composure and confidence, the steely Maple Leafs veterans pounced. In game seven, Joe Nieuwendyk who could barely bend to tie his skates let alone skate on them at times during the series, scored twice in the 4-1 win. Nieuwendyk was another one of the over-35 crowd picked up by general manager John Ferguson.

The Maple Leafs were confident, not cocky. They were quietly self-assured. Losses didn't rattle their emotions. Bad goals were shrugged off. Injuries became an annoyance, not an impediment or an excuse. The Toronto players simply

Toronto Maple Leafs

showed more guts and desire than the Senators.

In the media, the criticisms of the Senators' collapse tried to steal some of the credit away from the Maple Leafs team's fine effort. One commentator wrote of the Sens: "Having set the benchmark, having raised the bar oh so high, they achieved ... what many would have believed impossible — finding a novel and even more pathetic way to gag against the Toronto Maple Leafs in the Stanley Cup playoffs." Another was even nastier: "The lapdog Senators merited every bit of their playoff pooch reputation last night, hounded out of the post-season by the Maple Leafs for the fourth time in this millennium, a 4-1 game seven debacle."

There was a psychological impact of being on the losing end of the Battle of Ontario for the fans as well as the players. Some of the baser insecurities of Ottawa fans were brought out throughout the season. Despite having the superior team on paper, Ottawa set up their excuses. Call-in shows on Ottawa radio heard moans and complaints about the Maple Leafs. They were nothing more than a rich team from a rich city that was trying to buy its way to the Stanley Cup. The "poor" Senators had to go cap-in-hand to government officials annually. They had built their team through the draft, great scouting, and talent assessment. Many Ottawa boosters whined that the CBC, since it was headquartered in Toronto, showed an ingrained bias.

Leading up to the final regular-season meeting between the two teams in Ottawa, even Ottawa's city council got into

The Battle of Ontario: 2000-4

the poor-sport spirit. They passed a mock bylaw that outlawed Toronto Maple Leafs jerseys from the Corel Centre. (Toronto fans who ignored the bylaw would be taxed to the tune of a non-perishable food item for the local food bank.) The inferiority complex of colossal proportions seemed unbecoming of a sophisticated national capital with a fine hockey pedigree of its own.

The fourth episode of the Battle of Ontario was supposed to be a different story for the Leafs and the Senators for many reasons. The Sens had a new multi-billionaire owner in Eugene Melnyk, so the perpetual money woes of the team were finally resolved. They had abundant, multi-faceted talent on the ice. They had proven to everyone — or almost everyone — that they were a battle-hardened playoff team. In fact, they had taken the eventual 2003 Stanley Cup champions, the New Jersey Devils (coached by Pat Burns), to the seventh game of the Eastern Conference Finals. Fortunately, the Sens did not have to play Toronto that year in the playoffs.

In 2004, they were confident of their impending success. Before the regular season was three-quarters done, team captain Daniel Alfredsson, who was always the main target of criticism (besides Martin) after each playoff setback, boldly proclaimed that the Ottawa Senators were going to win the Stanley Cup this year. So Tucker's game and series-ending gesture of goodbye was particularly hard to swallow. Toronto had done it again — claimed the Battle of Ontario.

The sad truth for the Toronto Maple Leafs was that no

Toronto Maple Leafs

matter how dominant they'd been over Ottawa in the playoffs, they had neither won the Stanley Cup nor had they even made it to the finals for a long time. The farthest they had gone was the conference finals in 1999, Pat Quinn's first full season behind the Maple Leafs bench. Unfortunately, they had run into the only goaltender in the National Hockey League on a bigger roll than their Curtis Joseph — Buffalo's Dominik Hasek. Toronto had made it that far again in 2002 but a battered Leafs team ran out of gas against another improbable opponent, the Carolina Hurricanes, with future Leaf Ron Francis. The 2002 Leafs team was led by a man who played alongside Joe Nieuwendyk for the Calgary Flames when they won the Stanley Cup in 1989 — Gary Roberts. Back then, he was a gritty forward, but he was not known for being particularly thorough in his conditioning. After a near-career ending neck injury, however, he had transformed himself into a warrior, both in the gym and on the ice. He donned the Maple Leafs jersey in the summer of 2000.

It was no wonder Gary Roberts quickly became a fan favourite in Toronto. He was a local product who grew up in Whitby, mere minutes from the city's sprawling eastern boundary. He played as though he was always meant to be a Maple Leaf — a Maple Leaf from a bygone era. Though not as gifted in offense as Doug Gilmour, Roberts had the same sense of purpose and occasion. Like Gilmour, he had an instinct for when to take his game, and his team, to another level.

The Battle of Ontario: 2000-4

The 2001-02 post-season had been Gary Roberts's coming out party as a Maple Leaf. He became a true-blue hero by picking up the team on his surgically-repaired neck and shoulders and carrying them all the way to the Eastern Conference finals. He took over the mantle of offensive leadership from Mats Sundin, the team's injured captain and top scoring threat. Sundin would not return to action before well into the conference final series. Against the New York Islanders in the first round, Roberts scored key goals and levelled devastating bodychecks in one of the most physical series ever seen. He repeated his performance in the seven-game series win against the Senators.

The simultaneous signings of Roberts and another veteran, Shayne Corson, reflected the Pat Quinn (and Toronto Maple Leaf) philosophy that veteran leaders could inspire a team with their desire, fire, and work ethic. Corson played a key role. Against the Islanders, he rendered their star offensive player, Alexei Yashin, all but invisible by shadowing him for the entire seven-game series. Eventually the bumps and bruises caught up to Roberts in the series against Carolina. With seven regulars out of the lineup, and others playing at less than 100 percent, they lost the series and another chance to make the 2002 Stanley Cup finals.

Nonetheless, the Maple Leafs had reasserted themselves as a top-flight team by the first years of the 21st century. But they had not simply picked up where the Doug Gilmour crew left off. By 1996-97, the Toronto Maple Leafs hierarchy, particularly team owner Steve Stavro, had grown frustrated. Fletcher seemed unable to put together a team that could repeat the success of the 1992-93 and 1993-94 squads. The Toronto Maple Leafs, with their new Swedish superstar Mats Sundin (acquired for heart-and-soul captain Wendel Clark), had perhaps fooled everyone, including themselves, into thinking they really were an elite team.

First Burns, then a number of his players including Gilmour and Andreychuk, were shown the door by Maple Leafs brass. Eventually Fletcher left, too. The first face brought in to replace Fletcher was one very familiar to hockey fans around the world — Ken Dryden. Dryden had been born and raised in Toronto and therefore grew up with the legend that was the Maple Leafs. Although he had played for the Montreal Canadiens, the cerebral goalie-turned-lawyer was brought in to shore up the Leafs organization after a lacklustre 1996-97 season. Like Fletcher in 1991, Dryden added great credibility to the club. When he couldn't convince Bob Gainey to become Toronto's general manager, he brought in former Winnipeg Jets general manager Mike Smith as his assistant to do much of the work. Anders Hedberg became Dryden's assistant general manager. Bill Watters handled the team's contract negotiations. For the 1998-99 season, Dryden realized he also needed a top-flight coach — one who was adaptable and experienced. Pat Quinn, former president, general manager, and head coach of the Vancouver Canucks, fit the bill.

The Battle of Ontario: 2000-4

Dryden also stumbled upon another of his celebrated early moves in a late night food market. He ran into player agent Don Meehan, whose star free agent client, Curtis Joseph, was looking to leave Edmonton for a contending team with a high payroll. Toronto had only won 30 games in the previous season, but they had the building blocks in place for a serious run in a few years. A top-flight goalie to replace the injury-prone and inconsistent Felix Potvin was crucial. On July 15, 1998, the conversation that began in a market concluded with a four-year deal for Cujo and the resurgence of the Maple Leafs.

The team moved into their fancy new digs at the Air Canada Centre (ACC) in February, 1999. The arena, shared with the Toronto Raptors of the NBA and Toronto Rock lacrosse team, was modern, sleek, and efficient but also graceful and comfortable. The seating was designed to replicate the old Gardens' format as closely as possible. The ACC is considered to be one of the finest hockey buildings in the entire National Hockey League.

Unfortunately, repeating the pattern begun way back in the days of Eddie Livingstone and the Toronto Blueshirts, off-ice power-plays in the early 2000s made as many headlines as those on the ice. With all the experience and many egos in the new front office of Maple Leaf Sports and Entertainment Ltd., there was bound to be conflict. Eventually, Mike Smith resigned after losing a power struggle with Dryden and Quinn. Hedberg thought he would be promoted, but after

Toronto Maple Leafs

Dryden decided he didn't want the job or the title anymore, Quinn lobbied hard to become both the coach and general manager. By 2001, Pat Quinn was the only person in the NHL to be both a team's head coach and general manager. In the summer of 2003, Ferguson was finally hired, with Quinn's approval, to become the club's GM.

The Maple Leafs teams under the Dryden–Quinn regime made the playoffs each and every year and the Stanley Cup semi-finals twice. However, they could not stay away from injury or inconsistency long enough to win a Stanley Cup. Their consolation prize was that they were the hands-down winners of the Battle of Ontario.

In 2004, after another reshuffling of the ownership and management structure of Maple Leaf Sports and Entertainment, Dryden was moved to a less significant executive role. Eventually, he quit the company to run successfully as a federal Liberal candidate for a Toronto riding in the 2004 election.

The Toronto Maple Leafs club is once again at a crossroads. Although unable to win a Stanley Cup since 1967, the team has been competitive for the past decade. For a brief period in the early 1990s, and again at the turn of the millennium, Toronto was considered to be a top team. Fans of the Maple Leafs have been treated to sensational hockey by numerous star players wearing the team's uniform — Doug Gilmour, Grant Fuhr, Mike Gartner, Glenn Anderson, and Dave Andreychuk, as well as current superstars such as Gary

The Battle of Ontario: 2000-4

Roberts, Joe Nieuwendyk, Alexander Mogilny, Curtis Joseph, and Mats Sundin.

In years to come, in the next installment of the amazing story that is the Toronto Maple Leafs, these names will be welcomed alongside the great ones from the first 75 years of the team's existence. Dozens of former Leafs players have been elected to the Hockey Hall of Fame. From the early era came King Clancy, Hap Day, Syl Apps, Ted Kennedy, and Turk Broda. Afterwards, there was Red Kelly, Johnny Bower, Allan Stanley, Tim Horton, and Frank Mahovlich, as well as 1970s stars Lanny McDonald and Darryl Sittler.

The Toronto Maple Leafs won Stanley Cups in 1922 (as the St. Patricks), 1932, 1942, 1945, 1947, 1948, 1949, 1951, 1962, 1963, 1964, and 1967. The team's lengthy resumé sports many incredible highlights: Dye's "invisible" goal, the lucky bet that netted King Clancy, Bill Barilko flying through the air, Darryl Sittler breaking a record that may never be broken again, Rick Vaive scoring 50 goals three years in a row, and Doug Gilmour almost single-handedly returning pride and honour to a once-discredited franchise.

The amazing story of the Toronto Maple Leafs continues.

Bibliography

Batten, Jack. *The Inside Story of Conn Smythe's Hockey Dynasty.* Richmond Hill, Ont.: Simon and Schuster of Canada, 1970.

Batten, Jack. *The Leafs* (2nd Edition). Toronto: Key Porter Books, 1999.

Beddoes, Dick. *Pal Hal: A Biography of Canada's Most Controversial Sports Figure.* Toronto: Summerhill Press, 1984.

Brehl, Robert, ed. *The Best of Milt Dunnell: Over 40 Years of Great Sportswriting.* Toronto: Doubleday Canada, 1993.

Dupuis, David. *Sawchuk.* Toronto: Stoddart Publishing, 1998.

Fischler, Stan and Shirley. *Fischler's Hockey Encyclopedia.* New York: Thomas Y. Crowell Co., 1975.

Frayne, Trent. *It's Easy, All You Have To Do Is Win.* Don Mills, Ont.: Longmans Canada, 1968.

Hodge, Charlie and Howie Meeker. *Golly Gee It's Me!* Toronto: Stoddart Publishing, 1996.

Bibliography

Hockey Hall of Fame. *Honoured Members.* Bolton, Ont.: Fenn Publishing, 2003.

Holzman, Morey and Joseph Nieforth. *Deceptions and Doublecross.* Toronto: Dundurn Press, 2002.

Howe, Gordie and Colleen with Charles Wilkins. *After the Applause: Ten NHL Greats and Their Lives After Hockey.* Toronto: McClelland and Stewart, 1989.

Kendall, Brian. *Shutout: The Legend of Terry Sawchuk.* Toronto: Viking-Penguin Books of Canada, 1996.

Leonetti, Mike. *Maple Leaf Legends.* Vancouver: Raincoast Books, 2002.

McCrae, Earl. *The Victors and The Vanquished.* Toronto: Amberly House Ltd.

McDonald, Lanny. *Lanny.* Toronto: Random House of Canada, 1987.

McFarlane, Brian. *Clancy: The King's Story.* Toronto: ECW Press, 1997 (re-issue).

McFarlane, Brian. *Brian McFarlane's Wonderful World of Hockey.* Toronto: Stoddart Publishing, 2000.

Toronto Maple Leafs

McFarlane, Brian. *Stanley Cup Fever: 100 Years of Hockey Greatness*. Toronto: Stoddart Publishing, 1992.

McFarlane, Brian. *The Leafs: Brian McFarlane's Original Six*. Toronto: Stoddart Publishing, 1996.

McKinley, Michael. *Putting A Roof On Winter*. Vancouver: Greystone Books, 2000.

Meeker, Howie and Charlie Hodge. *Stop It There, Back It Up!* Toronto: Stoddart Publishing, 1999.

Podnieks, Andrew. *Return to Glory: The Leafs from Imlach to Fletcher*. Toronto: ECW Press, 1995.

Podnieks, Andrew. *Players*. Toronto: Random House of Canada, 2003.

Podnieks, Andrew. *The Blue and White Book*. Toronto: ECW Press, 1995.

Sittler, Darryl and Chris Goyens. *Sittler*. Toronto: McClelland and Stewart. 1991.

Smythe, Conn. *If You Can't Beat 'em In The Alley*. Markham, Ont.: PaperJacks Ltd., 1982.

Bibliography

Ulmer, Michael. *Captains*. Toronto: Seal Books-McClelland-Bantam Inc., 1995.

Williams, Dave. *Tiger*. Toronto. McClelland and Stewart-Bantam Ltd., 1984.

Young, Scott. *Heaven and Hell in the NHL*. Toronto: McClelland and Stewart, 1982.

Acknowledgments

How does one pick seven of the most significant moments in the history of one of the most storied teams in the history of Canadian sport? Very carefully.

The history of the Toronto Maple Leafs is replete with amazing events and amazing personalities, so narrowing it down to seven, one for each chapter, took a lot of negotiating between myself and hockey editor Stephen Smith. He should be commended for the courage in not only helping determine the final seven chapters, and the key events that would introduce them, but also in having the faith to bring on board a relative novice to this whole book-writing thing. I hope I have lived up to that esteem.

The seven key events are meant to be exciting touchstones, samples of the greatness that is the Toronto Maple Leafs' heritage. But those events were created by people: hockey players, both great and not so great, coaches, managers, and team owners. Many names were included in this book but because of the dearth of space, not every personality could be profiled. Many of the people discussed are no longer with us, passing on to that great hockey rink in the sky, but this book would not be as engaging as it is if not for the co-operation and generosity of time and spirit of a number of former Toronto Maple Leafs players.

Acknowledgments

The following Leaf alumni consented to original interviews for this project: Ron Ellis has been an amazing source of personal and professional inspiration for me for many years. He was always available for advice, a few quotes, or contact information for a retired NHLer. Mike Pelyk heads up the Maple Leaf Alumni Association at the time of the writing of this book and he too was very co-operative and a great source of information. Mark Osborne has been a pal for a number of years and is always generous with his time. Gus Mortson provided some great first-hand accounts of the Leafs dynasty of the 1940s, while Senator Frank Mahovlich took time out of his busy schedule to discuss the Over-The-Hill Gang of the 1960s. Allan Stanley, Terry Martin, and the incomparable Doug Gilmour were also kind to take time to speak with me for this project.

A number of interviews I had conducted at various points in my career were also consulted, with many of the quotes never seeing the light of day until this book. Those included a pair of interviews with former Maple Leafs captain Sid Smith who, tragically, died during the writing of this book. A classy man, full of integrity and humility, he will be missed. My previous conversations with Bill Derlago, Jim Morrison, Don Cherry, Doug Gilmour, Ron Ellis, Allan Stanley, Dick Duff, Mike Pelyk, and Wayne Carleton were also utilized.

On a personal note, my mom introduced me to the joy of reading very early on. My dad and grandparents have supported all of my endeavours, and this book would not have been possible without the support, love, patience, and proofreading of my lovely wife, Sheri.

Thanks to the crew of Altitude for the opportunity, and for doing their bit to bring Canadian history to the people.

Photo Credits

Cover: Frank Prazak / Hockey Hall of Fame; Graphic Artists / Hockey Hall of Fame: page 46; Imperial Oil – Lou & Nat Turofsky / Hockey Hall of Fame: pages 16, 30; London Life–Portnoy / Hockey Hall of Fame: page 58; Doug MacLellan / Hockey Hall of Fame: page 84.

About the Author

Jim Barber managed to find time to write this book while working as the Sports and Arts Editor for *The Barrie Advance*, and as the Editor for the *Collingwood-Wasaga Beach Connection*, two community newspapers in Central Ontario. Jim is a recipient of the Ontario Community Newspaper Association Award for Sportswriting and a Canadian Community Newspaper Award for editorial writing.

Educated at Trent University in Peterborough, Ontario, and Toronto's Centennial College, he has had a passion (obsession?) for hockey and hockey history most of his adult life. The books of Scott Young and Brian McFarlane inspired him as a youth, as do the works of Andrew Podnieks, Douglas Hunter, and Bruce Dowbiggin today. A member of the Society for International Hockey Research, current chairman of the Barrie Sports Hall of Fame Society, and executive member of the Collingwood Historical Society, Jim lives in a very old house, in a very small village called Nottawa, a few kilometres from the shores of Georgian Bay, near Collingwood, Ontario. He has a beautiful wife, two great stepsons, a somewhat annoying but loveable dog, an unnatural affinity for old hockey stuff, and way too many books on his bookshelves.

AMAZING STORIES
also available!

AMAZING STORIES™

CALGARY FLAMES
Fire on Ice

HOCKEY

by Monte Stewart

ISBN 1-55153-794-X

AMAZING STORIES
also available!

AMAZING STORIES™

OTTAWA SENATORS

Great Stories From The
NHL's First Dynasty

HOCKEY
by Chris Robinson

ISBN 1-55153-790-7

OTHER AMAZING STORIES

ISBN	Title	ISBN	Title
1-55153-959-4	A War Bride's Story	1-55153-951-9	Ontario Murders
1-55153-794-X	Calgary Flames	1-55153-790-7	Ottawa Senators
1-55153-947-0	Canada's Rumrunners	1-55153-960-8	Ottawa Titans
1-55153-966-7	Canadian Spies	1-55153-945-4	Pierre Elliot Trudeau
1-55153-795-8	D-Day	1-55153-981-0	Rattenbury
1-55153-972-1	David Thompson	1-55153-991-8	Rebel Women
1-55153-982-9	Dinosaur Hunters	1-55153-995-0	Rescue Dogs
1-55153-970-5	Early Voyageurs	1-55153-985-3	Riding on the Wild Side
1-55153-798-2	Edmonton Oilers	1-55153-974-8	Risk Takers and Innovators
1-55153-968-3	Edwin Alonzo Boyd	1-55153-956-X	Robert Service
1-55153-996-9	Emily Carr	1-55153-799-0	Roberta Bondar
1-55153-961-6	Étienne Brûlé	1-55153-997-7	Sam Steele
1-55153-791-5	Extraordinary Accounts of Native Life on the West Coast	1-55153-954-3	Snowmobile Adventures
		1-55153-971-3	Stolen Horses
		1-55153-952-7	Strange Events
1-55153-993-4	Ghost Town Stories	1-55153-783-4	Strange Events and More
1-55153-992-6	Ghost Town Stories II	1-55153-986-1	Tales from the West Coast
1-55153-984-5	Ghost Town Stories III	1-55153-978-0	The Avro Arrow Story
1-55153-973-X	Great Canadian Love Stories	1-55153-943-8	The Black Donnellys
		1-55153-942-X	The Halifax Explosion
1-55153-777-X	Great Cat Stories	1-55153-994-2	The Heart of a Horse
1-55153-946-2	Great Dog Stories	1-55153-944-6	The Life of a Loyalist
1-55153-773-7	Great Military Leaders	1-55153-787-7	The Mad Trapper
1-55153-785-0	Grey Owl	1-55153-789-3	The Mounties
1-55153-958-6	Hudson's Bay Company Adventures	1-55153-948-9	The War of 1812 Against the States
1-55153-969-1	Klondike Joe Boyle	1-55153-788-5	Toronto Maple Leafs
1-55153-980-2	Legendary Show Jumpers	1-55153-976-4	Trailblazing Sports Heroes
1-55153-775-3	Lucy Maud Montgomery		
1-55153-967-5	Marie Anne Lagimodière	1-55153-977-2	Unsung Heroes of the Royal Canadian Air Force
1-55153-964-0	Marilyn Bell		
1-55153-999-3	Mary Schäffer	1-55153-792-3	Vancouver Canucks
1-55153-953-5	Moe Norman	1-55153-989-6	Vancouver's Old-Time Scoundrels
1-55153-965-9	Native Chiefs and Famous Métis		
		1-55153-990-X	West Coast Adventures
1-55153-962-4	Niagara Daredevils	1-55153-987-X	Wilderness Tales
1-55153-793-1	Norman Bethune	1-55153-873-3	Women Explorers

These titles are available wherever you buy books. If you have trouble finding the book you want, call the Altitude order desk at **1-800-957-6888**, e-mail your request to: orderdesk@altitudepublishing.com or visit our Web site **at www.amazingstories.ca**

New AMAZING STORIES titles are published every month.